HARLEM GALLERY:

Book I, The Curator

Books by M. B. Tolson

RENDEZVOUS WITH AMERICA
LIBRETTO FOR THE REPUBLIC OF LIBERIA
HARLEM GALLERY: BOOK I, THE CURATOR

HARLEM GALLERY

Book I, The Curator

by

M. B. TOLSON

with an introduction by

KARL SHAPIRO

TWAYNE PUBLISHERS, INC.
NEW YORK

For

Ruth and Ruth Marie
Helen and Doris

Grateful acknowledgment for the reprinting of sections ALPHA, BETA, GAMMA, DELTA, EPSILON, and ETA is made to PRAIRIE SCHOONER; and, also, to POETRY for the excerpts from *E. & O. E.*, which won the Bess Hokin Award in 1952.

CONTENTS

INTRODUCTION

A great poet has been living in our midst for decades and is almost totally unknown, even by the literati, even by poets. Can this be possible in the age of criticism and of publication unlimited? It is not only possible but highly probable. Poetry today is an established institution which has many of the characteristics of a closed corporation. (One of the rules of the poetic establishment is that Negroes are not admitted to the polite company of the anthology.) Poetry as we know it remains the most lily-white of the arts. A novelist and pamphleteer like Baldwin is world famous; Tolson, easily the literary equal of any number of Baldwins, is less honored in his own country than the most obscure poetaster.

Yet not all poets and critics are at fault. Tolson has been recognized by eminent men of letters for a long time and at the extremes of the literary spectrum. Allen Tate paid homage to him in an introduction to LIBRETTO FOR THE REPUBLIC OF LIBERIA, an essay which is more famous than the poem. William Carlos Williams in the fourth book of PATERSON salutes him in this way:

> —and to Tolson and to his ode
> and to Liberia and to Allen Tate
> (give him credit)
> and to the South generally
> *Selah!*

Theodore Roethke, Selden Rodman, John Ciardi, Robert Frost, and Stanley Hyman have tried to bring Tolson to the general literary consciousness, but with little success.

In a time when Liberals are falling all over themselves to shake hands with Negroes, when a dusky maidenly model may even be hired for TV commercials, when black skin is the literary rage, poetry by Gentlemen of Color continues to be ignored. And it is ignored far out of proportion to the common indifference to the art.

It is one thing to accept an artist on the grounds of his art (regardless of race and creed) as long as the artist can adjust to the ruling "Graeco-Judaic-Christian" culture. It is another to accept an artist who contravenes that culture. Tolson belongs to the second category; he is in effect the enemy of the dominant culture of our time and place. He is, to use the term he prefers, an Afroamerican poet, not an American Negro poet accommodating himself to the Tradition. It is probably for this reason that the LIBRETTO, despite its *succès d'estime*, failed to tickle the sensibilities of the literati and professoriat. The LIBRETTO pulls the rug out from under the poetry of the Academy; on the stylistic level, outpounding Pound, it shocks the learned into a recognition of their own ignorance. HARLEM GALLERY pulls the house down around their ears.

Tolson writes in Negro. Walter Savage Landor told Thomas Hardy almost a century ago that English was a dying language. English poetry and Anglo-American poetry continue to bear out the dismal prophecy. The glorious shreds of English are in our century daintily stitched together by the campus Muse, while the new language undergoes all its multiple birth-pangs. England is the mother of our tongue but nobody knows who the fathers were or how many. It is a somewhat Chaucerian situation: bawdry, high learning, grammarlessness, history, myth all crying out for a jongleur or a poet.

It is not enough to equate Tolson, as his best critics have done, with Eliot or Hart Crane, the CANTOS or ANABASE. To make him equal is to miss the point, just as it would be to make him *better than*. Tolson writes and thinks in Negro, which is to say, a possible American language. He is therefore performing the primary poetic rite for our literature. Instead of purifying the tongue, which is the business of the Academy, he is complicating it, giving it the gift of tongues. Pound, Eliot, and Joyce did this, but with a pernicious nostalgia that all but killed the patient. Tolson does it naturally and to the manner born.

Here it is irrelevant to argue a thesis, but apropos to suggest common sense. The history of the American Negro places him linguistically at the center of the American culture, as it does no other nationality or "race." Negro survival has depended upon the mastery of the gradations of English; the Negro has in his possession a *Gradus Ad Parnassum* of our culture which no other minority or majority can conceivably encompass. This is the significance of Allen Tate's salute to Tolson's LIBRETTO. Only a Southern intellectual and poet would be in a position to welcome a Tolson, albeit at the white front door. Doc Williams, with his great intuitional spread of hands, takes in not only Tolson and Tate and Liberia but "the South generally!" One can practically feel the beat of Walt Whitman's wings against the dome of the Library of Congress.

The LIBRETTO FOR THE REPUBLIC OF LIBERIA speaks for itself and has been spoken of with courage and deep perception. Possibly it is too early for the assimilation of such a poem, even by poets.

The HARLEM GALLERY will not make matters easier. Massive as it is, it is only a beginning of a greater work, a kind of Odyssey of the American Negro, of which this is the prologue. The GALLERY returns to basic themes of the LIBRETTO. One of these is the accusation of Gertrude Stein that the Negro "suffers from Nothingness." Written in a style conforming to the ode form of the earlier poem, it is in fact a narrative work so fantastically stylized that the mind balks at comparisons. The milieu is Harlem, from the Twenties on. The dramatis personae comprise every symbolic character, from the black bourgeois babbitt and the Lenox Avenue poet to the alienated Negro Professor and sage who sits in the bar and elaborates, along with The Curator and others, a Platonic dialogue. The give-and-take ostensibly moves on a level of talk about the arts—a "floor" which is constantly caving in and plunging the reader into the depth of metaphysical horror which journalists nowadays refer to as the Race Question.

But like so many great works of poetry it is a comic poem. It is funny, witty, humoristic, slapstick, crude, cruel, bitter, and hilarious. The baroque surface of the poem modifies none of this. The HARLEM GALLERY is as if improvised by one of the great architects of modern poetry. It may be that this work, like other works of its quality in the past, will turn out to be not only an end in itself but the door to poetry that everyone has been looking for.

KARL SHAPIRO

HARLEM GALLERY:

Book I, The Curator

ALPHA

The Harlem Gallery, an Afric pepper bird,
awakes me at a people's dusk of dawn.
The age altars its image, a dog's hind leg,
and hazards the moment of truth in pawn.
The Lord of the House of Flies,
jaundice-eyed, synapses purled,
wries before the tumultuous canvas,
The Second of May—
by Goya:
the dagger of Madrid
vs.
the scimitar of Murat.
In Africa, in Asia, on the Day
of Barricades, alarm birds bedevil the Great White World,
a Buridan's ass—not Balaam's—between no oats and hay.

Sometimes a Roscius as tragedian,
sometimes a Kean as clown,
without Sir Henry's flap to shield my neck,
I travel, from oasis to oasis, man's Saharic up-and-down.

As a Hambletonian gathers his legs for a leap,
dead wool and fleece wool
I have mustered up from hands
now warm or cold: a full
rich Indies' cargo;

but often I hear a dry husk-of-locust blues
descend the tone ladder of a laughing goose,
        syncopating between
        the faggot and the noose:
        "Black Boy, O Black Boy,
        is the port worth the cruise?"

Like the lice and maggots of the apples of Cain
        on a strawberry tree,
        the myth of the Afroamerican past
        exacts the parasite's fee.

Sometimes the spirit wears away
        in the dust bowl of abuse,
like the candied flesh of the barrel cactus which
        the unpitying pitch
        of a Panhandle wind
        leaves with unpalatable juice.

Although the gaffing *"Tò tí?"* of the Gadfly girds
the I-ness of my humanness and Negroness,
        the clockbird's
        jackass laughter
        in sun, in rain,
        at dusk of dawn,
mixes with the pepper bird's reveille in my brain,
where the plain is twilled and the twilled is plain.

BETA

O Tempora,
what is man?
(Pull down the ladder of sophistry!)
O Mores,
what *manner* of man is this?
(Guy the ologists in effigy!)

Who knows, *without no,*
the archimedean pit and pith of a man?
(Ask the Throttler at Gîza!)
But if one seeks the nth verisimilar,
go to Ars by the way of Pisgah:
as the telescope of Galileo
deserted the clod to read the engirdling idioms of the star,
to the ape of God,
go!

But if one, a lotus eater, seeks
the umbrella of the green bay tree,
go to Solomon's seal—
to the ant's synecdoche.
To explore the troubled Virgin Pool *in* and *out* of man,
one needs the clarity
the comma gives the eye,
not the head of the hawk
swollen with rye.

O Heroics, O Pathetics,
what gives a figure in the fresco *Life* its stance?
Should my head escape a Herod's charger
after the Salomean dance,
let it go
(*non astutia, animo*)
with a frown nor a smile,
beyond the dust and ashes of tartufish guile.

The great god Biosis begets
the taste that sets apart
the pearls and olivets.

In *The Dialogue of Lees,*
a lee said, "The higher altitudes produce
the better teas."

As we, in a strange land, strangers, walked
beyond the Black Stone's colonnade,
the Amharic eunuch's voice
was hushed
like the embrace in an accolade:
"Great minds require of us a reading glass;
great souls, a hearing aid."
But I,
in the shuttlebox world,
again and again,
have both mislaid.

In the drama *Art*,
with eye and tongue,
I play a minor vocative part,
like the O
of St. Bridget when it is rent
by the basso profundo
in the abysmal D
of his fortissimo
descent.

So none shall ever censure me
because my emptiness grew as hard
as the tartar g in go,
nor, with a *beau geste* as white as a chard,
speed hyacinths to me
because, with a rival boast
(like that of the Thracian bard),
I lost my sight and voice
to the vanity of the Uppermost.

Among husks
in the crib of the psyche,
among chaff,
the jumping mice of anxiety, unable to stand the gaff,
tattle
a secret that knocks
no Lilliputian off his pegs:
"Hunter, O hunter,
let winter yellowlegs

strut and brattle—
in the if-of-things nothing is final
but the death rattle."

Like ironstone in its bed
or a fixed idea in the head
spin of a Ph. D.,
I am pegged as an ex-professor of Art:
from the start,
routine gored my identity—
a fore-
and-
aft
hat
tusked by a boar.
Ex sets me in my status: *formerly*
but not now;
and quoth the Raven, "Nevermore!"
In the Harlem Gallery,
not even a godling ism of Art rises up to bow to,
nor a horseshoe bias perches above the door.

My heart
nor
my head
turns a wheel of prayer
when certified Yeas and Nays are said
by pilgrim academics in the Babel of Art,
for the death of the quick
or the breath of the dead;

but within the flame is a core
of gas as yet unburnt
and undetected like an uninflected spoor.

Caviar I've eaten in many a vantage,
mulligan stew in many a retreat,
with Young Men labeled by their decades
The Lost, The Bright, The Angry, The Beat.

I was not gilded, like them,
with the gift of tongues.
Absent like shadow in Byzantine painting,
the upper rungs
of my ladder are zeros.

As a shoemaker
translates a second-hand boot,
each decade reshaped the dialects of
the owl's hoot,
the lamb's bleat,
the wolf's cry,
the hyena's laugh.
As serpents, sly,
The Lost, The Bright, The Angry, The Beat
(tongues that tanged bees in the head around the clock)
did not stoop the neck to die
like a dunghill cock.

GAMMA

The mecca Art is a babel city in the people's Shinar
with a hundred gates
and busybody roads
that stretch beyond all dates,
where sweating pilgrims fleshed in hallelujahs
jostle like cars in a bumping race;
and apostates
(sour chunks of fat
in a leviathan churning vat)
bob up and down,
bob to and fro,
to dodge, in a rain forest of phews,
the cobra's spit and the tiger's blow
apostles arrow at the face
in the name of dusty messiahs of the bethel place.

Like Caesar's Gaul,
like the papal tiara, tripartite,
the revolving stage of Experience,
at our midnight
show, downstages Heart and Hand and Soul—
each memorable in his immemorial role
in Veridic's *Human Comedy,*
where anther's nectar mixes with ox's gall.
We who are we
discover *altérité* in the actors on
the boards of the Théâtre Vie.

No catharsis homes:
no empathy calls:
synapses of the thinking reed snap
from too little reality
when the heavy dark curtain falls.

As the Utrillo of the Holy Hill *trans*figured
a *dis*figured Montmartre street
into a thing of beauty, to haunt
the unhaunted and the undaunted,
no Atropos said, "No-side"—so,
on the curve of a parallel detour,
nostalgia changes the fat and the gaunt
plug-uglies of our bygone selves,
shadowed and shadowing,
where
two fatheads and four flat feet
patrol the night watchman's beat.

Before he deserted the streets of Harlem,
and the fuel in his furnace died at curfew,
my Afroirishjewish Grandpa said:
"Between the dead sea Hitherto
and the promised land Hence
looms the wilderness Now:
although his confidence
is often a boar bailed up
on a ridge, *somehow*,

the Attic salt in man survives the blow
of Attila, Croesus, Iscariot,
and the Witches' Sabbath in the Catacombs of Bosio."

In salon, café, and studio,
from Greenwich Village to Montparnasse,
across the dialectic Alps from Dō to Dō,
my eyes and ears have shadowed the pros and cons
punctured with hot needles.
The *Closerie des Lilas!*
The *Café Voltaire!*
A magicked pageant beetles
along the horizon! Art is a harbor of colors
(with a hundred mosaic sail)
like Joseph's coat.

O hail
Paolo's doomsday *Sodom* that brasses
caricatures of patterns and colors and masses
fluxing away from the cruxing incandescence convulsing
the engouled town!
O hail
Tintoretto's *Paradise,*
lustrous and pulsing
with blue and silver,
red and ivory and brown!

DELTA

Doubt not
the artist and his age
(though bald as the pilled head of garlic),
married or divorced
and even vying downstage,
are both aware
that God or Caesar is the handle
to the camel's hair.

Ye weeping monkeys of the Critics' Circus
(colorless as malic acid in a Black Hamburg grape),
what profit it to argue at the wake
(a hurrah's nest of food and wine
with Auld Lang Syne
to cheer the dead),
if the artist wrought
(contrary to what the black sanders said)
for Ars',
the Cathedra's, or the Agora's sake?
No critic a Gran Galeoto
between the Art-lover and the work of art,
the world-self of the make-
believe becomes the swimming pool of a class,
the balsam apple
of the soul and by the soul and for the soul,
or silvered Scarahaeus glass
in which Necessity's *figuranti* of innocence and guilt
mirror themselves as they pass.

If brass,
in the name
of Id or Sinai or Helicon, wakes up the trumpet,
is it to blame?

Although
the moment's mistone
and the milieu's groan
sharp an unbearable ache
in the f of the age's bone,
this pain is only the ghost of the pain
the artist endures,
endures
—like Everyman—
alone.

The artist
is
a zinnia
no
first frost
blackens with a cloven hoof;
an eyeglass
—in the eye of a dusty wind—
to study the crosses and tangles in warp and woof;
an evergreen cherry
parasitic upon a winter sun;
a paltry thing with varicose veins
when the twelve fatigues are done.

Under the Lesbian rule of the seeress Nix,
blood and black bile
mix:
in the second of a bestiary-goat's caprice,
Élan,
the artist's undivorceable spouse
becomes
a Delilah of Délice
or
a Xanthippe bereft
of sonnets from the Portuguese.

In Chronos Park
the Ars-powered Ferris wheel revolves
through golden age and dark
as historied isms rise and fall
and the purple of the doctor's robe
(ephemeral as the flesh color of the fame flower)
is translated into the coffin's pall.

The St. John's agony
of the artist
in his gethsemane
without a St. John's fire—
the Vedic god of the snaky noose discovers;
his far far cry,
like the noise of block tin,
crackles the sky:

"Wayfaring man
unneighbored by
a wayfaring tree
(though one may rue
this bark of the Moreton Bay laurel),
it is true
a something *trans*-Brow or *cis*-Brow
—or both—
wills one to the wings of the eagle,
or to the teats of the sow.
Yet, no lip need sneer to the beard of an ape of God,
'Thou thing of no bowels, thou!'
So I say as the Sire
who chastens and rewards,
'Let thy blue eyes
resist white stars of red desire.' "

Like the shape of Africa,
the *raison d'être* of Art is a question mark:
without the true flight of the bat,
it is a hanker in the dark.
Not as face answers face in water,
but as windows answer each other,
one viewer,
lyrical as Hafiz in his cups,
discovers a lark;
his companion,
flat as an open Gladstone bag,
spies out an ark.

The blow of a fist on the nape,
this question came from a Dog,
"What color can escape
the fluky flues in the cosmic flux?"
Perhaps the high-C answer lies
in the wreck the sea sucks
back into her bowels. Let
the *Say* be said:
"In Philae the color is blue;
in Deir-el-Baheri, red;
in Abydos, yellow—
and these are by the ravens fed."

Art
is not barrel copper easily separated
from the matrix;
it is not fresh tissues
—for microscopic study—
one may *fix*:
unique as the white tiger's
pink paws and blue eyes,
Art
leaves her lover as a Komitas
deciphering intricate Armenian neums,
with a wild surmise.

EPSILON

The idols of the tribe,
in voices as puissant as the rutting calls
of a bull crocodile, bellow:
"We
have heroes! Celebrate them upon our walls!"

The frond of the walking leaf bends back,
discovers that (in the vanity
of Deir-el-Baheri frieze
and Savonnerie tapestry)
the spoors in the vein
of Art, indicative as uterine souffles, tail out a snide:
"From Dutch canals, not Siloam, came
the water in Rembrandt's pool
(as laughing Dogs confide);
and Milton's Lucifer was a Cavalier—
his God, a Roundhead
(in full career,
without an egghead to gibe):
dramatis personae of the ethos
miracled to befool
the hubris of the tribe."

O Lord of the House of Flies,
thy graven images of blood and class,
wise as the great horned owl of evil is wise,
infix the heart of an Ishmael
with the cold and yellow eyes

of the elite of serpent complexity:
the split-hair instant
that fear and blind choice verticalize
the venom fangs,
the ponderous coils bolting the cuneiforms
paralyze
(with the nonesuch of Pre-Cambrian artistry)
even a Michelangelesque imagination,
for its eternity.

O bulls of Bashan,
a nod from you is worse than a brief
from Diable Boiteux.
Just as a reef
at the head of a square sail
taken in or shaken out,
without fail,
regulates the size of the canvas,
a belief
shifted pro or shifted con,
as even the Dogs dare say,
fixes the four dimensions of A-is-A—
the center of gravity of the man inside.

A mute swan not at Coole, Beaufort's scale,
with the eerie mood of Bizan ware,
indicates a gale:
strange weather—strange
for a man or a mouse to make a change.

Again
by the waters of Babylon we sit down and weep,
for the pomp and power
of the bulls of Bashan
serve Belshazzarian tables to artists and poets who
serve the hour,
torn between two masters,
God and Caesar—
this (for Conscience),
the Chomolungma of disasters.

Again
we hang our harps upon the willows,
for the Ichabod and Sir Toby Belch of the olive leaf,
who,
lacking vitamin B,
lose an appetite for even grief.

Sicilian Bull and Sicilian Vespers
non obstante,
Art's
yen to beard in the den
deep down under root and stone
fossick gold and fossil ivory
stands out
like a whale's
backbone.

ZETA

My thoughts tilted at the corners like long Nepalese eyes,
I entered, under the Bear, a catacomb Harlem flat
(grotesquely vivisected like microscoped maggots)
where the caricature of a rat
weathercocked in squeals
to be or not to be
and a snaggle-toothed toilet
grumbled its obscenity.
The half-blind painter,
spoon-shaped like an aged parrot-fish,
hauled up out of the ruin of his bed
and growled a proverb in Yiddish.

His smiting stare
was a Carib's forefinger prizing
Vuelta tobacco leaves in the butt of a pipe.
No half-man disguising,
he wore his odds and ends
like a mandarin's worked gold
and seated image nodding in silk,
as his bold
thumb motioned me to an expendable chair.
His sheaf of merino hair
an agitated ambush,
he bottomed upon the hazard of a bed—sighing:
"The eagle's wings,
as well as the wren's,
grow weary of flying."

His vanity was a fast-day soup—thin, cold.
Through a glass darkly I saw the face
of a fantast, heard the undated voice of a poet crying,
among scattered bones in a stony place,
"No man cares for my soul!"

Perhaps the isle of Patmos
was like this.
Here emerges the imago
from the impotence of the chrysalis
in the dusk of a people's dawn—
this, this,
thought I as I gazed at his *Black Bourgeoisie*:
colors detonating
fog signals on a railroad track,
lights and shadows rhythming
fog images in a negative pack:
this, somehow, a synthesis
(savage—sanative)
of Daumier and Gropper and Picasso.
As a Californian, I thought *Eureka;*
but as Ulfilas to the dusky Philistines I said,
"Oh!"

Although
the Regents of the Harlem Gallery are as eye-
less as knitting needles, *Black Bourgeoisie*
(retching foulness like Goya's etching,
She Says Yes to Anyone)
will wring from their babbitted souls a Jeremian cry!

John Laugart,
alive beyond the bull of brass,
measured my interior—and said:
"A work of art
is an everlasting flower
in kind or unkind hands;
dried out,
it does not lose its form and color
in native or in alien lands."

Was he a radical leaf
created upon an under stem
at the behest
of the uncreated Diadem?
A fish of passage,
by hook unseen or crook unheard?
My curious art tried to gull his face,
the mug of a male umbrella bird,
haply black and mute.

This castaway talent
and I,
bent by paths coincident
on the lunar day
of Saint Crispin
(no matter how, by the heels, the land lay)
were fated to be
the Castor and Pollux of St. Elmo's fire,
on Harlem's Coalsack Way.

The Regents of the Harlem Gallery
suffer the carbon monoxide of ignorance
which—undetected in the
conference chamber—
leaves my budget as the
· corpse of a chance.

John Laugart
—a Jacob that wrestles Tribus and sunders bonds—
discovers, in the art of the issues
of Art, our pros, as well as our cons,
fused like silver nitrate used
to destroy dead tissues.

Derisive ha-has of the half-alive
may gird the loins of the soul,
or rive
the ribs of the mind.
Yet, in the
grime and the sublime
of illusion and reality
(among olivets and pearls),
sometimes irony
bends back the cues,
like a reflexive verb,
and gives the Gomorrhean blues
to the bulls of Bashan
that loose the full
butt of the bull
of blurb.

Again and again
huddled into a *cul-de-sac*
and skewed into sticks-in-the-mud
as to what shade of black
the villain Ultra should wear,
the dogs in the Harlem manger fret away their nails,
rake their hair,
initiate a game of pitch-and-toss;
then (wried by the seventh facial nerve) confuse
the T-shape of the gibbet with the T-shape of the cross.

Laugart's epitaphic words,
permanent as terre verte, are cooped
in my psyche.
A Bleak House grotesque,
his lower lip a drooped
whispering bell,
he wove—impressionistically,
like a Degas weaver,
and in a manner Gallic, *dégagé*—
coral stitches of the signature of an Ápelles
in his *pièce d'identité*:

"Since dish on dish of tripe often put
our master Rodin under a spell,
perhaps this bootleg liquor eclipses my will
as dram steps on the heels of dram;
yet, I shall never sell
mohair for alpaca
to ring the bell!"

At once the ebony of his face
became moodless—bare
as the marked-off space
between the feathered areas of a cock;
then, his
spoon-shape straightened.
His glance
as sharp as a lance-
olate leaf, he said:
"It matters not a tinker's dam
on the hither or thither side of the Acheron
how many rivers you cross
if you fail to cross the Rubicon!"

Postscript:
He was robbed and murdered in his flat,
and the only witness was a Hamletian rat.
But out of *Black Bourgeoisie* came—
for John Laugart—
a bottle of Schiedam gin
and Charon's grin
and infamy,
the Siamese twin
of fame.

ETA

Her neon sign blared two Harlem blocks.
In Aunt Grindle's
Elite Chitterling Shop
the variegated dinoceras of a jukebox
railed and wailed
from everlasting to everlasting:
Come back, Baby, come back—I need your gravy.
Come back, Baby, come back—I'm weak and wavy.
The talk of the town, I'm Skid Row bound—
and I don't mean maybe!

(O scholars)
this is the ambivalence of classical blues—and the
coins came from the blue-devils' pocket of Dipsy Muse.

Across an alp of chitterlings, pungent as epigrams,
Doctor Obi Nkomo
the alter ego
of the Harlem Gallery
—as a news-waif hallooed, "The Desert Fox is dead!"—
clicked his tongue
—a residual habit from the veld—
and
—stout as a peasant in the Bread-and-Cheese War—
said,
"The lie of the artist is the only lie
for which a mortal or a god should die."

Because nobody was a nobody to him,
when from his thin charcoal lips
irony escaped, it was malice toward none.
The therapy of his slips
by design into primitive *objets d'art*
humanized the patrons of the Harlem Gallery
as much as the masterworks
he salvaged from the Lethe
of the American Way in Black Manhattan.
Mr. Guy Delaporte III cried out before the Regents,
"Mr. Curator, what manner of man
is this?"

Unharassed by the *ignis fatuus* of a lost job,
Doctor Nkomo clicked throatily and, with a chuckle
whispered to me, "It's not this buckle-
head's right or wrong if he does right or wrong."
Like a humming disk came the strophe
of a rebel Bantu song.

Hubris is an evil the Greeks
(Euripides, Sophocles, Aeschylus)
boned and fleshed to wear the mask.
Pride is the lust-
sinewed wench the churchman speaks
of first in the Table of Deadly Sins:
Doctor Nkomo's *All hail to Man*
was a vane on the wing
to winnow the grain
in person, place and thing.

Too many (perhaps) of the Regents' corralled hours
Doctor Nkomo and I
left gored in bull rings of pros and cons:
without a horse-opera god, the Ultra dons
the matador's black of the wherefore and the why,
or hoists the white flag
and lets the red cells in the marrow die.

His *idée fixe* ebbed and flowed across the dinner table:
"Absurd life shakes its ass's ears
in Cendrars'—not Nkomo's—stable.
If,
anchored like hooks of a hag-fish to sea weeds
and patient as a weaver in haute-lisse tapestry,
a Rivera or a Picasso,
with a camel-hair alchemy,
paints in *fresco-buono*
the seven panels of a man's tridimensionality
in variforms and varicolors—
since virtue has no Kelvin scale,
since a mother breeds
no twins alike,
since no man is an escape running wild from
self-sown seeds—
then, no man,
judged by his biosocial identity
in toto
can be,
a Kiefekil or a Tartufe,
an Iscariot or an Iago."

Is philosophy, then, a tittle's snack?
History a peacock's almanac?
He laughed down at me,
a kidney without anchorage,
and said: "You must see through the millstone,
since you're not like Julio Sigafoos and me—
an ex-savage."

His ebony forefinger an assagai blade,
he mused aloud as the box played in Harlem's juke:
"Curator of the Harlem Ghetto, what is a masterpiece?
A virgin or a jade,
the *vis viva* of an ape of God,
to awaken one,
to pleasure one—
a way-of-life's aubade."

Black as cypress lawn,
the crag of a woman crabsidled in.
The breath of a fraxinella in hot weather,
her unlooked-for grin
evaporated; then,
like a well's spew
of mud and oil and raw gas,
she blew
her top.
Dipsy Muse slumped like Uhlan
when his feet failed to prop,
his squeal the squeal
of a peccary ax-poled in its pen.

                              The
                        stem and stern
                 of the Elite Chitterling Shop
                     pitched and ditched
      in the chatter and squawks, in the clatter and guffaws,
                            as a
                     Yarmouth yawl yaws
            when struck by a rogue-elephant sea.
            Scragged beyond the cavernous door,
            clamorous as a parrot against the rain,
            Dipsy Muse's vanity scrabbled in vain
      like an anchor along the neck-gorge of a sea-floor.
                       The jukebox
                     railed and wailed:
            The black widow spider gets rid of her man,
            gets rid of her daddy as fast as she can.
            If you fool around, I know what I'll do—
            like the black widow spider I'll get rid of you.
            A giraffine fellow whose yellow skin
            mocked the netted pattern of a cantaloupe
                  opened his rawhide pocketbook
                     to sniff of dope a whiff,
               with a galley curse and an alley gag;
      then—laughing, choking, brimstoning his spouse,
         he caved in like Ben Franklin's beggarly bag.
               Doctor Nkomo sighed:
      "The nicks and cuts under a stallion's tail
               spur him to carry it higher;
            but the incised horsetail of a man
         drains the bones of his I-ness drier."

A black outsider with all his eggs but one
in the White Man's basket, he quaffed his beer,
stretched his beanpole legs;
                    then
—a rubberneck Robin Hood in a morris dance—
readied a hobby with another color for a ride
beyond the Afrikaner's stance.
"O Romeo," he said, "O Casanova,
prithee, what is chivalrous—what, barbaric?
(Why gnaw one's thoughts to the bone?)
When a caveman painted a rubric
figure of his mate with a gritstone,
Eros conquered Thanatos."

His eyes glistening dots of an ice plant,
he said: "My Western friends
—with deserts to be turned into green pastures—
rent diving bells to get the bends,
curfew morals, incubate tsetse flies,
stage a barroom brawl of means and ends
in a *cul-de-sac*.
(Eagles dying of hunger with cocks in their claws!)
That rebel jukebox! Hear the ghetto's dark guffaws
that defy Manhattan's Bible Belt!
Aeons separate my native veld
and your peaks of philosophy:
I made the trek, Curator,
on Man's vegetable ivory,
in threescore years and ten."

A whale of a man, I thought; *a true,*
but not a typical, mammal.
He absorbs alien ideas as Urdu
Arabic characters.

In a sepulchral corner, I glimpsed
a Scarlet Sister Mary on the make,
her lips dark and juicy like a half-done T-bone steak.

The giraffine fellow eyed us with a dog-ape look
and outed his impatience in a sigh;
a single-acting plunger
cast the die,
"Mister, *who* are you?"
His catarrhal eye
baited by Doctor Nkomo's hair
(the silvery gray patina of a Japanese alloy),
he was but a squeaking Cleopatra boy
when the reply
came like the undershot of a Poncelet water wheel:

"Obi Nkomo, my dear Watson; but that is nil,
a water stair that meanders to no vessel. If you ask
what am I, you dash on rocks the wisdom and the will
of Solon and Solomon.
Am I a bee
drugged on the honey of sophistry?
Am I a fish from a river Jordan,
fated to die as soon as it reaches an Asphalt Sea?"

Not a sound came from
the yellow giraffine fellow—
not a sound
from the bowels
of this Ixion bound
to the everlasting revolving ghetto wheel.

Nearer the ground than Townsend's solitaire,
Doctor Nkomo
raked his hair
. . . his brain . . .
but he did not blink the cliff of ice.
"*What* am I? *What* are you?
Perhaps we
are twin colors in a crystal.
When I was a Zulu
lad, I heard an old-wives' tale
for seven-foot-spear Chakas to be.
In a barnyard near a buffalo trail
a hunter discovered an eagle
eating dung with chickens.
He carried the feathered rex to a mountain top,
although it raised the dickens.
The hunter explained, 'You're not a chicken, Aquila.'
He launched the ungainly bird into space.
A fouled umbrella!
In the wing lock
of habit, it tumbled in disgrace
. . . down . . . down . . . down . . .
a ghostified cock!

"Out of the visaing face
of the sun swooped the falcon baron
clarioning the summons of an aeried race.
Twice
the barnyard eagle answered the Solar City wight;
thrice
he spiraled the simoom-blistered height—
braked and banked and beaked
upward, upward, into transfiguring light.
Old Probabilities, *what* am I?
Mister, *what* are you?
An eagle or a chicken come home to roost?
I wish I knew!"

His character (in the Greek sense)
phrased a nonplus—needed a metaphor's
translation. As an African prince,
kings and chiefs peacocked themselves
behind him;
and he, himself tough-conscienced, had slain
heathenism, the Giant Grim,
without a backward cry.
Scot and plot,
caste and class,
rifted right angles to the curving grain.

The dream of Abraham's bosom bottled long ago,
he walked the Pork Barrel's porphyry
street with the man in the ears;
and the glassy

rivers of talk
—Heraclitean, Fabian, Marxian—
in the lights and shadows of the illuminating gas,
bona fides,
limned a figure and cast
of *Homo Aethiopicus* who knew
all riverine traffickers pass
beyond the Seven Walls of Water—to join
. . . the Last of the Greeks . . .
of the Romans, the Last.

Once in a while
his apology
shaped itself like the symbol
Q
in a skipper's log.
During the falconry
in the chamber of the Regents,
Mr. Delaporte III flew
off at a tangent and off the handle.
Doctor Nkomo's Dandie Dinmount terrier
epithet sprang
across the tables.
My gavel big-talked in slang.
Like a turtle's head,
the session withdrew
into its shell.
The old Africanist bowed cavalierly and said:
"I've called the gentleman a liar
—it's true—
and I am sorry for it."

Wealth of the fettered,
illth of the lettered,
left his realism, like rock dust, unweathered:
one who eyes
the needle of the present to knit the future's garb.
In his own buttoned guise
he seemed to speak to the man Friday in Everyman
boned and lined and veined
for the twelve great fatigues to the Promised Land:

"The golden mean
of the dark wayfarer's way between
black Scylla and white Charybdis, I
have traveled; subdued ifs in the way;
from *vile-canaille* balconies and nigger heavens, seen
day beasts and night beasts of prey
in the disemboweling pits of
Europe and America,
in the death-worming bowels of
Asia and Africa;
and, although a Dumb Ox (like young Aquinas), I
have not forgot
the rainbows and the olive leaves against the orient sky.

"The basso profundo
Gibbon of Putney
—not the lyric tenor, Thomas of Celano—
hymns the *Dies Irae!*"

THETA

In the *château en Espagne* of Vanity,
Bones and Flesh,
Black Keys and White Keys
—Changs and Engs—
argued themselves into apoplexy.

Their hostess,
the Marquise de Matrix,
panged by the pall
of a tribulating moment,
like a Duchess of Malfi at a grand ball,
oiled the waters:

"Something there is in Art that does not love a wall.
Idea and image,
form and content,
blend like pigment with pigment
in a flesh color.
What dread hand can unmix
pink and yellow?
Even a nixie says, 'Nix!'
The weight and fineness of a work of art,
like a sample coin,
must pass *the trial of pyx*.
In spite of an age's smile or frown,
the perennial tooth of this esthetic truth
grows at the root as it wears away at the crown."

Montague's son and Capulet's daughter
the tryst-
ing tree of Art unites
as the wrist
the hand and arm—
unites them as the miracle of the metaphor smites
disparate realms into a form
tighter than a mailed fist.

Ye knights of the Critics' Circus,
why tilt at the fetish
of a sophistry?
Nature and Art,
rejuvenating as the Cybele
to whom we sing *Non Nobis—*
Nature and Art,
dedicated to oneness,
ignore
the outer and the inner
of a person, a place, a thing;
and both alma maters,
eyes unbridled,
explore
the whole of the *rete mirabile*:
the freedom of figurate counterpoint in a
flying fugue or fleeing flea,
the coat of a nucellus,
the testa of a seed,
the integument of a Paltock's flying Indian
can be removed by only the claws of a naked need.

No guinea pig of a spouse
to be cuckolded in a mood indigo,
no gilded in-and-out beau
to crackle a *jeu de mots* about the house—
Art, the woman Pleasure, makes no blind dates,
but keeps the end of the tryst with one;
she is a distant cousin of aeried Happiness
the lovebird seeks against the eye-wrying sun,
in spite of her fame,
dubious as Galen's sight
of a human body dissected,
in spite of the *hap* in her name,
ominous as a red light.

The claw-thrust
of a rutting tigress,
the must
of a rogue elephant—
these con the bull of predictability,
like Happiness,
a capriccio bastard-daughter of Tyche.

KKK, the beatnik guitarist, used to say
to High Yellah Baby
(before he decided to rub
out the light of his eyes
in the alley of Hinnom behind the Haw-Haw Club):
"The *belle dame*—Happiness—the goofy dream of
is a bitch who plays with crooked dice
the game of love."

IOTA

The hour with the red letter stumbles in:
Doctor Nkomo and I counterpoise beside
ebony doors of the Harlem Gallery,
Hrothgarian hosts,
closemouthed and open-eyed.
He winks at me, bows to
each ohing, ahing guest
among the gobbler-breasted matrons and their spouses
whose busheled taxes tax strange interludes of rest.

His wits in their Sunday best,
he wears the mask and grins, "Aloha!"
(Please excuse
the beachcomber's ambiguity of this,
which puzzles the Cadillac Philistines.)
Yet none need lose
his good right eye like Agib, who
let curiosity lead him amiss.

From nightingales of the old Old World,
O God, deliver us!
In the Harlem Gallery, pepper birds
clarion in the dusk of dawn
the flats and sharps of pigment-words—
quake the walls of Mr. Rockefeller's Jericho
with the new New Order of things,
as the ambivalence of dark dark laughter rings
in Harlem's immemorial winter.

The East Wing's
rigors and vigors in varicolors,
broods of the ethos and artistic moods,
range from sea level to peak altitudes,
like the cluster of the pinaster.
Ironies and tensions of flesh
going to grass,
paeans and laments of identities
signed in the thought and felt hinterlands of psyches—
now impasted and sprayed and fixed
with waterglass
on dry plaster.
Unlike the teeth of the parrot-fish
fused into a single mass,
polychromatic *heres* and *theres,*
juxtaposed, image the
oddly odd or oddly even
of reality and fable.
Purse pride
of neither gold, nor silver, nor brass,
from porcelain tray and handled sable
fig leaf and barebone in water colors
echo the monastic archetypes
of a haunted master,
or,
facing fate-fating
Now,
subdue the accents, vivify the nuances
of success and disaster.

The West Wing
is no belt of calms:
in the midst of its dramatis personae,
the listening ear can hear,
among the moderns, blue
tomtoms of Benin;
the seeing eye can see fetishes unseen,
via
rue Fromentin and Lenox Avenue.

Painters consecrated like the Brescian Blackamoor
on a holyday
or amused like Somerscales (the eternal naïf)
in his owling way
fetch from streets that have no eyes
and alleys that have no lips
the antique and the newly-made
in our *cis*-Apocalypse.

The sable and camel's-hair
incarnate in oils
an upstage of faces as unsoiled as irisated rain
or repulsive like purulent boils;
a downstage of faces as madder-bleached as dry bones
on an alkali plain
or fissured like agueweeds
in a marsh's toils;
a backstage of faces as empty as a mistigris
or bedeviled like a sea dog's prelithic visage
when the stays lean amiss.

The North Wing's
burnt-in portraits
(colors mixed with wax and resin and verve
liquefied with heat that sings)
enmesh Negroid diversity—
its Kafiristan gaucherie,
its Attic wit and nerve.
This is Harlem's Aganippe
(not America's itching aitchbone)
where characters, flat and round,
project a rhythm, a mood, a scene, a tone.
Sometimes beyond the bourgeois Greek
and yet within the pale,
variegated colors, like those of the agate snail,
blend with the white and yellow
of beaten eggs that mix the juice
from the tender roots of the Smyrna-fig to fellow
light and shadow, line and curve,
grown mellow.

All shapes and sizes and colors of boots
from the ape-cobbler's last
for every actor in the Harlem cast
entertain, absorb, or vex
as the egg trot in the design
goes awry or toes the line
while trafficking,
in the human comedy,
with *Bios* and *Societas* and *X*
as well as the divine.

The South Wing's
orientations of dusky Lion Hearts
(in fresco and secco),
who find
on Toynbee's frontiers
their counterparts,
loom in the varied habiliments of health and blight—
bizarres and homespuns
in a cacophony of colors
as if courage had a copyright.

The idols of the tribe,
in voices as puissant as the rutting calls
of a bull crocodile, bellow:
"We
have heroes! Celebrate *them* upon our walls!"

Heralds' College
(the sceptre's y-fretted retreat;
and, like the Order of the White Eagle,
obsolete)
is dubbed by Doctor Nkomo
afterwit's aftermeat.
He likes to retrek
the vanitied souterrains of history;
puzzle out the kings and queens,
the bishops and knights,
on Prince Eugene's
greenhouse chessboard of heredity.

He chuckles:
"If
a Bourbon should shake his family tree
long enough . . . he
—beyond a Diogenic doubt—
would kneel at the mourners' bench,
dressed in black crepe,
as cannibal and idiot,
rapist and ape,
tumble out."

These Lion Hearts (then) are unsynchronized opposites,
gentlemen and galoots
from Afroamerica;
tone colors of the triple-octaved xylophone
Daddy Blue Note plays on black-letter days;
seven against Thebes
in seven-league Afroamerican boots;
voices of the voiceless
—like the *Iliad*, the *Gilgamesh*, the *Divine Comedy*—
obelized
now and then
by a dusky Origen,
but authentic as a people's autography.

However, this immaturity,
like the stag tick's,
will disappear
like its wings,
when it settles upon a red red deer.

O dry bones of Highgate,
Phidias and Van Gogh and Aristophanes,
Shakespeare and El Greco,
Velasquez and Cervantes,
Orozco and Dante and Pissarro—
all these
(Olympians wombed in the Vale of Tears)
fleshed stout on
the bee bread of self and the beef of history,
like Balzac, the *de*-fetishist, who,
deaf to the phews of irony,
surpasses the Zolas, old and new,
in frescoes of bourgeois reality.

KAPPA

Mr. and Mrs. Guy Delaporte III,
through the shifting maze of Harlem's Vanity Fair,
oh and yawn and ah their way:
mismatched oddlegs:
he,
with a frown like curd;
she,
with a smile like whey.

An Atlantean S
neons
Mr. Delaporte's Success
as President of Bola Boa Enterprises, Inc.,
which left its competitors,
long ago . . . long ago,
dead as the figure of Christ
in a *mortorio*.

His
soul of gold,
like the Ark's mercy seat,
Mr. Guy Delaporte III is the symbol
of Churchianity
at Mount Zion,
the bethel of the Sugar Hill elite—
say the valley people of Mount Sinai
as they wash each other's feet.

When Professor Freez Skerritt's whiskyfied baritone
gropes along the bars of *Sweet Mystery of Life*,
all alone, all alone,
Mr. Delaporte's wonder twills, like surah silk,
about it and about.
Unable to lead his wife
(with her incurves and outcurves of breasts and hips)
captive,
he weeps like Alexander the Fire Burnt Out
because
no brand-new $-world in Harlem gives him pause.

Now,
Hagar's son,
to escape the bone mill of the *ultima ratio*,
needs the agility
of the grand galago.

Before the *bête noire* of John Laugart's
Black Bourgeoisie,
Mr. Guy Delaporte III takes his stand,
a wounded Cape buffalo defying everything and Everyman!
Above and about
Mrs. Delaporte hovers Bishop Euphorbus Harmsworth,
the shield of Sobieski.
Since Doctor Nkomo is one
no harlot of Hush Hush ever gave dead tongue,
among the topsyturvy pros and cons of our patrons,
in a North Wing alcove
he halters me:

"Is it not
the black damp of the undisturbed pit
that chokes the vitals—damns the dream to rot?
The bane of the hinterland,
as well as the outland,
is the mirage of the Status Quo.
No platinum black in the undifferentiated sand.
My village? The *fera* unmanned
in *homo faber*. Alkali water after a rain-
less simoom. Stagnant
blood in a dead-end vein.
Dialectics?
The midwife of reality.
The cream separator of life.
The sieve, Curator, of wheat and chaff.
So, let our eyes,
like Mohammed's,
disappear in the guise
of a crocodile laugh!"

A hurt sea dog, I cut his deck of metaphors:
"On its shakedown cruise,
the *Black Bourgeoisie* runs aground
on the bars of the Harlem Blues."

Doctor Nkomo quicks the quid of an analogy:
"This work of art is the dry compound
fruit of the sand-box tree,
which bursts with a loud report
but scatters its seeds quietly."

We have dined too long, O Harlem, with Duke Humphrey!
In the kitchen,
the chef, I, mixes black and yellow and red
images, leaves You at the table
with brown bread
and the ghost of the thing
unsaid:
Give voice to a bill
of faith at another hour.
My humor is ill.
A night like this, O Watchman,
sends a Derain to Weimar
to lick the Brissac jack boots
of Das Kapital that hawks things-as-they-are.
Then O then, O ruins,
I remember
the alien hobnails
of that cross-nailing Second of September
did not crush like a mollusk's shell,
in café and studio,
the *élan* of Courbet, Cézanne, and Monet,
nor did the self-deadfall of the Maginot
palsy the hand of Chagall,
Matisse,
and Picasso.

LAMBDA

From the mouth of the Harlem Gallery
came a voice like a
ferry horn in a river of fog:

"Hey, man, when you gonna close this dump?
Fetch highbrow stuff for the middlebrows who
don't give a damn and the lowbrows who ain't hip!
Think you're a little high-yellow Jesus?"

No longer was I a boxer with a brain bruised
against its walls by Tyche's fists,
as I welcomed Hideho Heights,
the vagabond bard of Lenox Avenue,
whose satyric legends adhered like beggar's-lice.

"Sorry, Curator, I got here late:
my black ma birthed me in the Whites' bottom drawer,
and the Reds forgot to fish me out!"

His belly laughed and quaked
the Blakean tigers and lambs on the walls.
Haw-Haw's whale of a forefinger mocked
Max Donachie's revolutionary hero, Crispus Attucks,
in the Harlem Gallery and on Boston Commons.
"In the beginning was the Word,"
he challenged, "not the Brush!"
The scorn in the eyes that raked the gallery
was the scorn of an Ozymandias.

The metal smelted from the ore of ideas,
his grin revealed all the gold he had stored away.
"Just came from a jam session
at the Daddy-O Club," he said.
"I'm just one step from heaven
with the blues a-percolating in my head.
You should've heard old Satchmo blow his horn!
The Lord God A'mighty made no mistake
the day that cat was born!"

Like a bridegroom unloosing a virgin knot,
from an inner pocket he coaxed a manuscript.
"Just given Satchmo a one-way ticket
to Immortality," he said. "Pure inspiration!"
His lips folded about the neck of a whiskey bottle
whose label belied its white-heat hooch.
I heard a gurgle, a gurgle—a death rattle.
His eyes as bright as a parachute light,
he began to rhetorize in the grand style
of a Doctor Faustus in the dilapidated Harlem Opera House:

King Oliver of New Orleans
has kicked the bucket, but he left behind
old Satchmo with his red-hot horn
to syncopate the heart and mind.
The honky-tonks in Storyville
have turned to ashes, have turned to dust,
but old Satchmo is still around
like Uncle Sam's IN GOD WE TRUST.

Where, oh, where is Bessie Smith
with her heart as big as the blues of truth?
Where, oh, where is Mister Jelly Roll
with his Cadillac and diamond tooth?
Where, oh, where is Papa Handy
with his blue notes a-dragging from bar to bar?
Where, oh, where is bulletproof Leadbelly
with his tall tales and 12-string guitar?

Old Hip Cats,
when you sang and played the blues
the night Satchmo was born,
did you know hypodermic needles in Rome
couldn't hoodoo him away from his horn?
Wyatt Earp's legend, John Henry's, too,
is a dare and a bet to old Satchmo
when his groovy blues put headlines in the news
from the Gold Coast to cold Moscow.

Old Satchmo's
gravelly voice and tapping foot and crazy notes
set my soul on fire.
If I climbed
the seventy-seven steps of the Seventh
Heaven, Satchmo's high C would carry me higher!
Are you hip to this, Harlem? Are you hip?
On Judgment Day, Gabriel will say
after he blows his horn:
"I'd be the greatest trumpeter in the Universe,
if old Satchmo had never been born!"

MU

Hideho Heights
and I, like the brims of old hats,
slouched at a sepulchered table in the Zulu Club.
Frog Legs Lux and his Indigo Combo
spoke with tongues that sent their devotees
out of this world!

Black and brown and yellow fingers flashed,
like mirrored sunrays of a heliograph,
on clarinet and piano keys, on cornet valves.

Effervescing like acid on limestone,
Hideho said:
"O White Folks, O Black Folks,
the dinosaur imagined its extinction meant
the death of the piss ants."

Cigarette smoke
—opaque veins in Carrara marble—
magicked the habitués into
humoresques and grotesques.
Lurid lights
spraying African figures on the walls
ecstasied maids and waiters,
pickups and stevedores—
with delusions
of Park Avenue grandeur.

Once, twice,
Hideho sneaked a swig.
"On the house," he said, proffering the bottle
as he lorded it under the table.
Glimpsing the harpy eagle at the bar,
I grimaced,
"I'm not the house snake of the Zulu Club."

A willow of a woman,
bronze as knife money,
executed, near our table, the Lenox Avenue Quake.
Hideho winked at me and poked
that which
her tight Park Avenue skirt vociferously advertized.
Peacocking herself, she turned like a ballerina,
her eyes blazing drops of rum on a crêpe suzette.
"Why, you—"
A sanitary decree, I thought. "Don't *you* me!" he fumed.
The lips of a vixen exhibited a picadill flare.
"*What* you smell isn't cooking," she said.
Hideho sniffed.
"Chanel No. 5," he scoffed,
"from Sugar Hill."
I laughed and clapped him on the shoulder.
"A bad metaphor, *poet*."
His jaws closed
like an alligator squeezer.
"She's a willow," I emphasized,
"a willow by a cesspool."
Hideho mused aloud,
"Do I hear The Curator rattle Eliotic bones?"

Out of the Indigo Combo
flowed rich and complex polyrhythms.
Like surfacing bass,
exotic swells and softenings
of the veld vibrato
emerged.

. . .

Was that Snakehips Briskie
gliding out of the aurora australis of the Zulu Club
into the kaleidoscopic circle?

. . .

Etnean gasps!
Vesuvian acclamations!

. . .

Snakehips poised himself—
Giovanni Gabrieli's
single violin against his massed horns.

. . .

The silence of the revelers was the arrested
hemorrhage of an artery
grasped by bull forceps.
I felt Hideho's breath against my ear.
"The penis act in the Garden of Eden," he confided.

. . .

Convulsively, unexampledly,
Snakehips' body and soul
began to twist and untwist like a gyrating rawhide—
began to coil, to writhe
like a prismatic-hued python
in the throes of copulation.

Eyes bright as the light
at Eddystone Rock,
an ebony Penthesilea
grabbed her tiger's-eye yellow-brown
beanpole Sir Testiculus of the evening
and gave him an Amazonian hug.
He wilted in her arms
like a limp morning-glory.
"The Zulu Club is in the groove," chanted Hideho,
"and the cats, the black cats, are *gone!*"

In the *ostinato*
of stamping feet and clapping hands,
the Promethean bard of Lenox Avenue became a
lost loose-leaf
as memory vignetted
Rabelaisian I's of the Boogie-Woogie dynasty
in barrel houses, at rent parties,
on riverboats, at wakes:
The Toothpick, Funky Five, and Tippling Tom!
Ma Rainey, Countess Willie V., and Aunt Harriet!
Speckled Red, Skinny Head Pete, and Stormy Weather!
Listen, Black Boy.
Did the High Priestess at 27 rue de Fleurus
assert, "The Negro suffers from nothingness"?
Hideho confided like a neophyte on The Walk,
"Jazz is the marijuana of the Blacks."
In the *tribulum* of dialectics, I juggled the idea;
then I observed,
"Jazz is the philosophers' egg of the Whites."

Hideho laughed from below the Daniel Boone rawhide belt
he'd redeemed, in a Dallas pawn shop,
with part of the black-market
loot set loose
in a crap game
by a Yangtze ex-coolie who,
in a Latin Quarter dive below Telegraph Hill,
out-Harvarded his Alma Mater.

. . .

Frog Legs Lux and his Indigo Combo
let go
with a wailing pedal point
that slid into
Basin Street Blues
like Ty Cobb stealing second base:
Zulu,
King of the Africans,
arrives on Mardi Gras morning;
the veld drum of Baby Dodds'
great-grandfather
in Congo Square
pancakes the first blue note
in a callithump of the USA.
And now comes the eve of Ash Wednesday.
Comus on parade!
All God's children revel
like a post-Valley Forge
charivari in Boston celebrating the nuptials of
a gay-old-dog minuteman with a lusty maid.

. . .

Just as
the bourgeois adopted
the lyric-winged piano of Liszt in the court at Weimar
for the solitude of his
′aeried apartment,
Harlem chose
for its cold-water flat
the hot-blues cornet of King Oliver
in his cart
under the
El pillars of the Loop.
. . .
The yanking fishing rod
of Hideho's voice
jerked me out of my bird's-foot violet romanticism.
He mixed Shakespeare's image with his own
and caricatured me:
"Yonder Curator has a lean and hungry look;
he thinks too much.
Such blackamoors are dangerous to
the Great White World!"
. . .
With a dissonance
from the Weird Sisters,
the jazz diablerie
boiled down and away
in the vacuum pan
of the Indigo Combo.

NU

Rufino Laughlin
(M. C.)
peacocked to the microphone
as a fixed-on grin lighted his corrugated face
like the island pharos of King Ptolemy.

The M. C. raised his hand,
Rufino Laughlin raised his voice,
in rococo synchronization.
"Ladies and Gents," he demosthenized,
"the Zulu Club has a distinguished guest tonight
who has never let us down.
In a thousand years,
when the Hall of Fame
lies in ruins on genesis-ground,
the poems and the name
of Hideho Heights,
the poet laureate of Lenox Avenue,
will still be kicking around.
Let Harlem give a great big hand,
therefore and *henceforth,*
to a great big poet and a great big man!"

A boiler—a caravan boiler
of applause
exploded.
My thoughts wandered and wondered
... *the poet is no Crusoe in the Zulu Club* ...

His nightly nightmare waterlooed,
the M. C.'s histrionic antics
drooped and crinkled:
leaves of a Bermuda onion
with yellow dwarf.

Colorful as a torch lily,
her hips twin scimitars,
a tipsy Lena
who peddled Edenic joys
from Harlem to the Bronx
plucked the poet's filamentous sleeve and begged:
"If you make me a poem,
Hideho,
I'll make you my one and only daddy-o
till the Statue of Liberty
dates
a kinkyhead."

The poet was no Gallio
who cared for none of these;
so he tossed his palm slap into her buttocks.
Her wiggles were whisky-frisky.
"You're a *female* woman," he said,
grave as the falling accent of a Cantonese scholar; and then
the soul seemed to pass out of the body as he announced,
"Sister, you and I belong to the people."
The tipsy Lena's
giggles were the wiggles
of a coral fish's spinal fin
when it poisons and kills the alien next of kin.

XI

Hideho Heights,
a black Gigas,
ghosted above us
in a fan vaulting of awkward-age lights and shadows.

Sudden silence,
succulent as the leaves of a fat hen, swallowed
up the Zulu Club.

He staged a brown pose that minded me
of an atheistic black baritone
who sang blue spirituals that turned
some white folk white, some pink, and others red.

Hideho's voice was the Laughing Philosopher's
as he said:
"Only kings and fortunetellers,
poets and preachers,
are born to be."

In spite of the mocker's mask,
I saw Hideho
as a charcoal Piute Messiah
at a ghetto
ghost dance.

Does a Yeats or a beast or a Wovoka
see and hear
when our own faculties fail?

Was it *vox populi*
or the Roman procurator
who said to the
Roman who was not a Roman,
"Much learning doth make thee mad"?

In a faraway funereal voice,
Hideho continued:
"The night John Henry was born
no Wise Men came to his cabin, because
they got lost in a raging storm
that tore
the countryside apart
like a mother's womb
when a too-big son is born."

"Great God A'mighty!"
cried Dipsy Muse,
as his arm went halfway round
the calf's-foot
jelly mound
of the Xanthippean spouse
whom the whim
of Tyche
had created in the image
of Fatso Darden.
The Birth of John Henry!
Murmurs ebbed and flowed:
soughing sounds
in the ears of a stethoscope.

. . .

The night John Henry is born an ax
of lightning splits the sky,
and a hammer of thunder pounds the earth,
and the eagles and panthers cry!

. . .

Wafer Waite—
an ex-peon from the Brazos Bottoms,
who was in the M.-K.-T. station
when a dipping funnel
canyoned the Cotton Market Capital—
leaps to his feet and shouts,
"Didn't John Henry's Ma and Pa
get no warning?"

Hideho,
with the tolerance of Diogenes
naked in the market place on a frosty morning,
replies:
"Brother,
the tornado alarm became
tongue-tied."

. . .

John Henry—he says to his Ma and Pa:
"Get a gallon of barleycorn.
I want to start right, like a he-man child,
the night that I am born!"

. . .

The Zulu Club patrons whoop and stomp,
clap thighs and backs and knees:
the poet and the audience one,
each gears itself to please.

Says: "I want some ham hocks, ribs, and jowls,
a pot of cabbage and greens;
some hoecakes, jam, and buttermilk,
a platter of pork and beans!"

John Henry's Ma—she wrings her hands,
and his Pa—he scratches his head.
John Henry—he curses in giraffe-tall words,
flops over, and kicks down the bed.

He's burning mad, like a bear on fire—
so he tears to the riverside.
As he stoops to drink, Old Man River gets scared
and runs upstream to hide!

Some say he was born in Georgia—O Lord!
Some say in Alabam.
But it's writ on the rock at the Big Bend Tunnel:
"Lousyana was my home. So scram!"

. . .

The Zulu Club Wits
(dusky vestiges of the University Wits)
screech like a fanfare of hunting horns
when Hideho flourishes his hip-pocket bottle.

High as the ace of trumps,
an egghead says, " 'The artist is a strange bird,' Lenin says."
Dipping in every direction like a quaquaversal,
the M. C. guffaws: "Hideho, that swig would make
a squirrel spit in the eye of a bulldog!"

Bedlam beggars
at a poet's feast in a people's dusk of dawn counterpoint
protest and pride
in honky-tonk rhythms
hot as an ache in a cold hand warmed.
The creative impulse in the Zulu Club
leaps from Hideho's lips to Frog Legs' fingers,
like the electric fire from the clouds
that blued the gap between
Franklin's key and his Leyden jar.
A Creole co-ed from Basin Street by way of
Morningside Heights
—circumspect as a lady in waiting—
brushes my shattered cocktail glass into a tray.
Am I a Basilidian anchoret rapt in secret studies?
O spiritual, work-song, ragtime, blues, jazz—
consorts of
the march, quadrille, polka, and waltz!
Witness to a miracle
—I muse—
the birth of a blues,
the flesh
made André Gide's
musique nègre!

· · ·

I was born in Bitchville, Lousyana.
A son of Ham, I had to scram!
I was born in Bitchville, Lousyana;
so I ain't worth a T.B. damn!

· · ·

My boon crony,
Vincent Aveline, sports editor
of the *Harlem Gazette,*
anchors himself at my table.
"What a night!" he groans. "*What* a night!"
. . . I wonder . . .
Was he stewed or not
when he sneaked Hideho's
Skid Row Ballads
from my walk-up apartment?
Then the You advises the I,
Every bookworm is a potential thief.

. . .

Ma taught me to pray. Pa taught me to grin.
It pays, Black Boy; oh, it pays!
So I pray to God and grin at the Whites
in seventy-seven different ways!

I came to Lenox Avenue.
Poor Boy Blue! Poor Boy Blue!
I came to Lenox Avenue,
but I find up here a Bitchville, too!

. . .

Like an explorer
on the deck of the *Albatross,*
ex-professor of philosophy, Joshua Nitze,
sounds the wet unknown;
then, in humor, he refreshes the Zulu Club Wits
with an anecdote on integration,
from the Athens of the Cumberland:

"A black stevedore bulked his butt
in a high-hat restaurant
not far from the bronze equestrian statue
of Andrew Jackson.
The ofay waitress hi-fied,
'What can I do for you, Mister?'
Imagine, if you can, Harlem nitwits,
a black man mistered by a white dame
in the Bible Belt of the pale phallus and the chalk clitoris!
The South quaked.
Gabriel hadn't high-Ced his horn,
nor the Africans invaded from Mars.
It was only the end-man's bones of Jeff Davis
rattling the *Dies Irae*
in the Hollywood Cemetery!
The Negro dock hand said,
'Ma'am, a platter of chitterlings.'
The ofay waitress smiled a blond dolichocephalic smile,
'That's not on the menu, Mister.'
Then the stevedore sneered:
'Night and day, Ma'am,
I've been telling Black Folks
you White Folks ain't ready for integration!' "

The hilarity of the Zulu Club Wits
(unconsecrated like blessed bread)
grows as public as the paeans of Artemis.
The Sea-Wolf of Harlem sneers: "Uncle Tom is dead;
but keep a beady eye on his grandson, Dr. Thomas—
minister without portfolio to the Great White World!"

In two hours
Vincent Aveline will plane South
to fly-fish for sepia baseball stars.
In the skull-shaped mugs
the concocted *Zulu Chief* arrests my eye—
for its legend as an aphrodisiac
out-Marathons Jotham's fable;
but the quixotism that plays
hide and fox in Everyman
incites me to lift my glass.
"Partner, one for the road!"
Aveline becomes enisled for a lost moment.
"Damon," he jives,
your Pithias needs a *Zulu Chief.*"

Later . . . later . . . he
says something startling
as the toast "Drink! Live!"
inscribed on the gold glasses
among the skeletons of the Catacombs:
"Just caught my wife and Guy Delaporte III
between the sheets
of his Louis XIV bed!
A Black Diamond stool pigeon puked it up."
I feel the silence of the *omertà* oozing in.

. . .

Black Diamond,
heir presumptive to the Lenox Policy Racket,
kindles,
with igniting lines from Hideho's *Flophouse Blues,*

the sticks and twigs of greed
on the hearth of his flyaway Jezebel,
whose body, done in the yellow of Minyan pottery,
was exposed and rhapsodized and caricatured
as Miss Bronze America,
to the envy and pride and lust of the
black and tan, black-and-blue, black and white,
in the Harlem Opera House—so Black Diamond says,
"Baby, I play any game that you can name,
for any amount that you can count."

His ego lionized
in the first, second, and third person,
Black Diamond flags down and highballs
Tom, Dick, and Harry—
controls them as
a single stop knob
a set of reed pipes
in an organ.

It was I who taught Black Diamond
his first lesson in the Art of Picasso's Benin,
at Waycross, Georgia—
aeons before Africa uncorked an uppercut:
many a *tour de force* of his
executed in Harlem dives and dead ends
has greened the wide-awake eyes
of such masters as
Giglio and Gentile,
Bufalino and Profaci.

O schoolmasters,
living and half-alive and dead,
the Zulu Club
is not the fittest place to recall,
by fits and starts,
Seneca's young Nero
. . . and . . .
Aristotle's youthful Alexander!

And Black Diamond, now
dwarfing me at my table,
vilifies the Regents of the Harlem Gallery;
swears, on his Grandma's family Bible,
that the sons-of-bitches
had better not fire his beloved teacher,
because his stool pigeons
have dedicated to him
a dossier on *each* and *every one* of the bastards!
And the only reason he doesn't flip the red-hot stuff to
Walter Winchell
(that great truth-serum guy)
is because he has Race Pride,
as a life-member of Afroamerican Freedom, *Incorporated.*
Anyway, he hates to see Race skeletons that whoopee a stink
in top-hat closets dumped in Times Square—
since White Folks are always ready to disinfect the privy
of decent Black Folks like me and him.
Then, too, if an ace boss squeals
in the blackjack game of his free enterprise,
it sets a bad example—*bad* for the little guys!

His Grandma used to dingdong a scripture,
"By their tails ye shall know 'em."
That's the reason he planks down his church dues,
at Mt. Sinai, a year in advance.
You see,
if a fluke flunks in his free enterprise
and the Sweet Chariot swings low, the preacher can't blab
at the biggest funeral in Harlem
and St. Peter can't gab
to the Lord God A'mighty
that Black Diamond's record was in the red—like
a Red editor's among gnawing bellies in Greenwich Village.
. . . Then, too . . .
it's a good example for the little guys.

He jots down
six private telephone numbers
and goads the open sesame deep into my breast pocket.
The gapers are all eyes,
like the tubers of the Jerusalem artichoke.
"Curator," he grins, "you'll never have to turn
on a slab in a morgue and say to Black Diamond,
'Is *that* you, Brutus?' "

Tom, Dick and Harry,
pigmied by the ghetto Robin Hood
(innocuous *now* as a basking shark),
catch the cue, double up like U-bridle irons inverted, and
let loose
geysers of guffaws.

At neighbored tables
the Zulu Club Wits
rant in circles for, against, about
This and *That*.

Shadrach Martial Kilroy
president of Afroamerican Freedom,
his skin soft and moist
like a salamander's,
waxes apocalyptic:
"The White Man is the serpent
in Dolph Peeler's *Ode to the South*."

The Sea-Wolf of Harlem,
Lionel Matheus,
apostatizes:
"To continue the symbolism,
your Afroamerican is the frog I saw
in a newspaper illustration:
the harder the frog tugged outward,
the deeper it became impaled
on the inward-pointing fangs of the snake."

Doctor Nkomo says: "The little python would not let go
the ass of the frog—so the big python swallowed both."
I seem to sense behind the masks of the Zulu Club Wits
thoughts springing clear of
the *terra firma* of the mind—
the mettled forelegs of horses
in a curvet.

Mr. Kilroy's nose,
broad and compressed
as the tail of a salamander,
tilts upward at the ends
in the scrouge of his indignation;
all of a sudden
the promontory of his belly
quakes with cultivated jollity,
like effeminate grains of wet quartz.

"Lionel Matheus," he
pontificates,
"to carry your symbols to a Sublime Porte—
you need to see, you son of a Balaam,
the unerring beak,
the unnerving eye,
the untiring wing,
of Afroamerican Freedom, *Incorporated*—
the Republic's secretary bird."

The gape of Lionel Matheus, a nut-brown Mirabell,
is wider than the eye in the leach of a sail;
then, the image of Agrippa must have buoyed
into his mind, for he says mockingly,
"Almost thou persuadest me to be a nigger-lover."

Mr. Kilroy sighs out his fatigue,
"It is hard for a phobic camel to go
through the eye of a needle of truth."
Metaphors and symbols in Spirituals and Blues
have been the Negro's manna in the Great White World.

Apropos of something or nothing,
Doctor Nkomo interposes:
"Nationalism,
the Sir Galahad of the African republics, has
severed the seventh
tentacle of the octopus of imperialism."

Every hail-fellow-well-met
in propria persona
because of
the white magic of John Barleycorn,
the Zulu Club Wits
become
absent
like the similes in the first book of the *Iliad*,
or
ugly
like the idiom the Nazarene spoke,
or
tight
like ski pants at the ankle.

Hideho Heights,
slumped in the shoal of a stupor,
slobbers and sobs,
"My *people*,
my people—
they know not what they do."

OMICRON

"Life and Art," said Doctor Nkomo, "beget incestuously
(like Osiris and Isis)
the talented of brush and pen.
Artistic instinct draws,
on a rock in the Kalahari Desert,
a crocodile for Bush-born men.
Without Velasquez and Cranach,
what would Picasso be?
Or Léger without Poussin?
Or Amedeo Modigliani without Sandro Botticelli?"

Design trailed design as a scroll saw capered in his mind:
Is *Homo Aethiopicus* doomed,
like the stallion's beard,
to wear the curb of the bridle?
The melon feeds the imago of the ladybird
in the Diadem's diapered plan:
the heritage of Art
—no Triboulet in the tragedy *Le Roi s'amuse*—
nurtures everywhere
the wingless and the winged man.

Unseen,
perhaps,
unheard,
low heels will overtake high heels,
to reach the never-never travelers' rest,
a democracy of zooids united by a stolon
but separated by a test.

An artist makes what he can;
every work of art asserts,
"I am that I am."
So leave the rind to the pedant
and the bone to The Hamfat Man.

O Time, O Customs,
how can an artist make merry
in the tenderloin's maw,
unless he add a head and a wing and a claw
to the salamander of Gerry?

The age,
taut as the neck of a man on a gallows tree,
demands
a Friar Bacon who will cast
a head of brass
to clarion, "Time is,
Time was, Time is past,"
before the graven image topples,
breaks in pieces,
while the necromancer snuggles deep
between the breasts
and in the arms
of the courtesan Sleep.

It is an age that ties
tongues and stones irises;
and no leper cries,
"Unclean! Unclean!"

The idols of the tribe
make the psyche of the artist lean
inward like an afferent blood vessel,
or turn its view
—an adjusting iris diaphragm—
toward the backyard of the Old
or the front yard of the New.

As a skiascope views the changes
of retinal lights and shadows,
the élan-guided eye, in good time, ranges
a land of the leal
that no longer estranges.

In the magnetic field of Art, the creed
of the exploring coil discovers
diatonic nuances of taste
and vintage varieties that need
no philter for lovers.

The net loss of the artist
is
the alms of the rich—
the vice
that consoles the *hoity-toity*
but leaves
the pocketbook of his art
the poorer.

The net profit of the artist
is
the art-fetish delivered
from the black hole of the flesh
by the mercy of the knife.

The pride of the artist
is
the leach of green manure
that slows down
the sleet and snow and ice
of an age's scorn.

The élan of the artist
is
the rain forest sapling
which pushes upward
through bog and snarl
to breathe the light.

The school of the artist
is
the circle of wild horses,
heads centered,
as they present to the wolves
a battery of heels,
in the arctic barrens where
no magic grass of Glaucus
gives immortality.

The grind of the artist
is
the grind of the gravel in the gizzard
of the golden eagle.

The temperament of the artist
is
the buffer bar of a Diesel engine
that receives the impact
of a horizontal of alpine and savanna
freight cars drawn along in the rear.

The sensibility of the artist
is
the fancier of the Brahman and Hamburg and Orington,
the Frizzle and Silky—but
everlastingly he tests to discover
new forms and strange colors,
nor does he balk to wring the neck
of Auld Lang Syne
in any breed.

The esthetic distance of the artist
is
the purple foxglove
that excites
the thermo receptors of the heart
and the light receptors of the brain.

PI

Omega is not *I like*.
In the class chaos under the Order
of *Homo Caucasicus,*
the artist must not barter
the law of measure, the will to refrain,
as the withering chrysanthemum trafficks its water
for rain:
flowers made of hummingbird feathers
the Zoological Gardens in Regent's Park contain.

Even when
his world is ours and ours is his—
a lodestar that leads into its ring
two kingdoms with colors and shapes and textures in high
relief under a single king—
even then
the artist, like a messiah, is egoistic
and the work of art, like the art of God,
is a rhyme in the Mikado's tongue to all save the hedonistic.

Image-breaking?
Perhaps,
to the euclidean; but,
to the perspectivist
—in the curved space of aeons of cultures—
the mixed chalice and wafer bread
may become as dead
as the dead spindles of lathes.

A work of art is a domain
        (mediterranean)
    of *this* race,
    of *that* time,
    of *this* place,
    of *that* psyche,
    with an Al Sirat of its own—
and, beyond its bridge to Paradise, the ritual of
        light and shadow,
        idiom and tone,
        symbol and myth,
    pleasures the lover of Art alone
in a bourne where no grapes of wrath are sown.

    Without a limitation as to height,
    a work of art is a peak in Anthropos
    (low as Soufrière or high as Kilimanjaro)
    with the temper (sometimes) of a volcano
    made by an ape-god of Eros or Thanatos.
        O son of profits,
    when does the hour come to sight
    the anchor? When will the parasitic crater
    stifle the bulls of Bashan in the night?

    O ye of the Samson Post,
        let the remembrance
        of things past
        season with tolerance
        the pigs in baskets.

Is not the stifle shoe
placed on the sound leg
of a stallion to strengthen the weak?
Therefore,
let us beg
in the court of error
no ape of God for a fool,
although
the scriptures of Art
(schools within school)
be
as esoteric, pluralistic, contradictory
as texts of the *Koran*,
the *Book of the Dead*,
the *Bhagavad-Gita*,
the *Vulgate*,
whose disciples
(tempers fermented to a head
like yeasted malt)
babble in the babel of debate
for eternity and a day,
garb heretics in garments
painted with flames and figures of devils
to be led
to the *auto-da-fé*.

Doctor Obi Nkomo said
in his address before the artists
of the Market Place Gallery in Harlem:

"Remember
the Venerable Yankee Poet
on the unfamiliar red carpet of the Capitol
as he visaed the gospel of the Founding Fathers
. . . *Novus Ordo Seclorum* . . .
spieled by every dollar bill.
Remember
Paul Cézanne,
the father of modern Art,
a Toussaint L'Ouverture of Esthetics.
Remember
a genius is not a fence-sitter
with legs wide apart,
a tree crow between
a true crow and a jay.
. . . Remember, yes, remember . . .
Zola, Renoir, Degas, Gauguin, Van Gogh, and Rodin
hailed Cézanne;
but *vox populi* and red-tapedom
remained as silent as spectators in a court
when the crier repeats three times, 'Oyez!' "

Sometimes
a critic switches the dice and gambles on
his second sight,
since the artist's credo is
. . . *now* a riding light . . .
then a whistling buoy in
a Styx' night.

(The Harlem Gallery, too, was grieved by Bunyan's
                    crabtree cudgel
         when Doctor Nkomo threw a stinkpot into
                 the Market Place Gallery,
   among Black Muslims and artists and Good White Friends.
           "The Critics' Circus grants an artist
                       a passport to
          the holy of holies," he said, "or a whorehouse;
                     but never to
       Harpers Ferry or Babii Yar or Highgate.")

            The critic is an X stopper pausing
                  between a work of art
          and the electromagnet wave causing
                    the listening ear
                   to ring and smart.

    I visit a work of art: in the garden How
       I pluck the pansy; blink the weed;
    fish in the dark tarn Auber for the Why;
     seek out the What and trace its breed.

                 The road to Xanadu
       is not a jack-o'-lantern of the Hamburg grape.
                  God is not mocked
                   (nor is His ape),
             for, while our Goliath laves
               in aloes and frankincense,
         the harlot Now the master paints
        aspires to hang in the gallery Hence
              with Brueghel's knaves
               and Cimabue's saints.

RHO

New Year's Day
Hedda Starks telephoned me
from a Harlem police station.
Her fit of laughing and crying was as convulsive
as the heehaws of a Somaliland she-ass.
So the desk sergeant
waxed human. He juggled the receiver and swore
Hedda was a horned screamer,
as she agonized in her cell at midnight:
"O sweet Jesus,
make the bastard leave me alone!
I'll call The Curator
—the son-of-a-bitch—
and send 'im to Big Mama to get the goddamn rubbish!"

Verbatim was to Sergeant Ghirlandaio
what a glasshouse is to a plant.
"I hope I'm not in Harlem," he said,
"when St. Peter opens the books on Judgment Day."
His chuckle was the impish mockery of an echo
in the bottomless canyon of Hesiod's
—and our—
Brazen Age.

Hedda Starks, alias Black Orchid,
was a striptease has-been
of the brassy-pit-band era—
but listen, Black Boy, to the hoity-toity scholars:
"A vestige is rarely, if ever, present in a plant."

Mister Starks
hailed from Onward, Mississippi—
via Paris, Texas, *via* Broken Bow, Oklahoma.
How he got his *Christian* name is a legend
that tickles the inwards of the Zulu Club Wits.
When he was four years old,
his black mother took him to
the Big House on an *ante-bellum* estate;
and the Lady wanted to know the baby's name
and the proud mother said "Mister."
Since every Negro male in Dixie was
either a *boy* or an *uncle,*
the mistress turned blue and hot
like an arc-welder's torch.
"A pickaninny named *Mister?*" the old doll hissed;
and the maid, slamming the mop bucket down,
screamed: "Miss Leta,
it's *my* baby and I can name it
any damn thing I please!"

The first time Mister Starks, the piano-modernist
of the Harlem Renaissance, lamped
Black Orchid at the Bamboo Kraal,
her barbarian bump and sophisticated grind
(every bump butted by the growl of a horn)
played, with him, the witch,
like the serpentine belly dance
of Congo Leopold's Cleo de Merode, which
captivated Anatole France.

The intelligentsia of Mister's bent
became Hedda's steps on the aerial ladder
of the black and tan bourgeoisie;
but her exhumed
liaison with Mr. Guy Delaporte
(in the *Harlem Emancipator*)
was like the red kimono
that broke Woodrow Wilson's heart.

Did a sibyl say to Aeneas,
"The descent to Avernus is easy"?

Well, Mister Starks needed no Hindu mystic
mulattoed in Atlanta
and
turbaned in Harlem
to tell him—*that*.

And, contrary to what the Cumaean divined,
it was no labor, no task,
for Mister to escape to the upper air:
it was a *beau geste*,
Hardyesque—
fit for the limelight of the Harlem Opera House
in the auld lang syne of Charles Gilpin,
the most
sinister-smiling
of the Emperor Joneses
inspired by the root of evil.

SIGMA

On a red letter day
pained by the sharp ache of a corn
that protests a tight shoe,
the Angelus Funeral Home received,
by registered mail,
the last will and testament of Mister Starks.

Ma'am Shears, LL. B. and owner,
of long sight, of short breath,
spelled out the letter three times.
Her memory hooked a feather, a wing and a fin:
Mister Starks was to be buried in the tails he'd worn
the night the Harlem Symphony Orchestra
premiered his *Black Orchid Suite;* and
his ebony baton, the gift of a Dahomean witchdoctor,
was to be poised in his hand; and
Hedda Starks was to be exhorted
to turn over to The Curator of the Harlem Gallery
the MS., *Harlem Vignettes,*
which the aforesaid person
(Hedda Starks, alias Black Orchid)
had possessed
with malice aforethought.

Miss Ester Bostic,
the late Dr. Igor Shears' medical secretary,
pieced together the archetype for newsmongers.
Her hobby was making checkerwork
with her fingers or with her lips.

She is now Ma'am Shears' bookkeeper
and *dame de compagnie*
to Trinidad
on the widow's annual forget-me-not pilgrimage
to the twin tombstones that transfigure
the grave of Igor Shears
and the grave-to-be of Ma'am Shears. (But let
us get on with the classic version of the Zulu Club Wits.)
. . . And now . . .
the volatile Miss Bostic
became fixed mercury
as Ma'am Shears,
her arms the flukes of a wounded whale,
swept aside Mr. Abelard Littlejohn—
the springbok impresario of the Angelus Funeral Home.

The pince-nez the third of his six ex-wives had given him,
on St. Valentine's Day,
clattered—broken and unnoticed—upon
the late Dr. Igor Shears' bust
of Frederick Augustus Douglass.
Puffing like Hedley's
Puffing Billy in 1818,
Ma'am Shears grabbed the telephone
and dialed Mister Starks' tenement-room.
"The fool!" she said compulsively. "The fool!"
She'd resurrected his threat to commit suicide
in a scene (in a Sugar Hill juke) that out-Hamleted the
Gloomy Dane.

As he talked with her,
no sign of illness of mind revealed itself
like the twist of a billiard ball.
He was still the highbrow composer,
and his replies came like the answers
at the intervals of a fifth in a fugue.

"Mister, don't try it!" she begged.
"Try it?" he laughed. "I'm a Hannibal—not a Napoleon."
The cryptic words were blisters
along the course of a nerve.
She recalled Reverend Thigpen's subject, *Love of Life*,
two Sundays ago at Mt. Zion.
Sweat trickled down her yellow cheeks.
"It's not like Black Folks to commit suicide."
Her voice sank in a chuckle
as thick as the mother of vinegar.
"Aren't we civilized yet?" he scoffed.
Ma'am Shears groaned, "Civilization and suicide?"
"Soil and plant," he said. "Masaryk speaking—in Vienna."

Mister Starks,
airy as a floating lily pad,
said: "Ma'am Shears,
I want you and Mr. Abelard Littlejohn,
the merry widow-killer of the Angelus Funeral Home,
to meet me
(and the late Dr. Igor Shears)
at Archangel Gabriel's hangout
on Elysian Boulevard.
Au revoir!"

Whiter than Pliny's white
black, Ma'am Shears faced
the end in smoke.

"Angels can do no more,"
Miss Bostic oraculized.

Ma'am Shears
heaved and set the sigh of an old she-walrus
after a futile mating bout.

"This means headlines and $'s for Angelus,"
Miss Bostic finessed
with clicks of her Tru-Grip teeth.

Her spirit
the depressed abdomen of a shrimp,
Ma'am Shears sank upon
her haunches
in her pillowed reclining-chair.

Sergeant Ghirlandaio,
who knew his Conan Doyle from *aardvark* to *zythum,*
discovered a bullet in Mister's heart.
But it was the supt.
who found the .38 hidden in
Crazy Cain's toilet bowl.

. . . New Year's Day . . .
. . . in a Harlem jail . . .
Hedda Starks—alias Black Orchid,
arrested at a marijuana party
and haunted in her cell—
turned over the MS., *Harlem Vignettes*,
to The Curator
and made her peace with God.

O spindle of Clotho,
O scroll of Lachesis,
O scales of Atropos,
the black ox treads the wine press of Harlem!

TAU

The MS., *Harlem Vignettes,*
was done up in a mamba's skin.
On a side along the spine, a snake's head
arrowed a legend inscribed in purple-red ink:
"In the sweat of thy face shalt thou make a work of art."

A snapping turtle on its back,
my memory jumped:
in his youth, Mister Starks had published
a volume of imagistic verse.

... Even in this last manuscript ...
Sanson's images of my own Harlem
burned brightly
like gold and silver paper
at a Chinese funeral.

On the title page
Mister had scribbled:
"I should have followed—perhaps—*Des Imagistes*
down the Macadam Road.
But I'm no Boabdil
at the Last Sigh of the Moor."

So let Tyche pluck, Black Boy, a few oysters
from a planter's bed—a site located in Harlem
strewn with layers of shells, slag, cinders, gravel,
where Art shouts:
"We must shoot General Aupick!
Garrote Guizot's imperative *Enrichissez-vous!*"

UPSILON

Mister Starks: A Self-Portrait

My talent was an Uptown whore; my wit a Downtown pimp:
my boogie-woogie record, *Pot Belly Papa*,
by Alpha & Omega, Inc., sold a million discs.
(God help *vox populi—vox Dei!*)
I etch, here and now, a few
of the everybodies and somebodies and nobodies
in Harlem's *comédie larmoyante*.
John Laugart said: "A work of art is a moment's
antlers of the elaphure in the hunting lodge of time."

I am no neutral—carbon in fats.
Like the Fathers of Oratory,
I am not bound by a vow.
Sometimes I'm sunk like a ha-ha-wall.
So what the hell?
Am I not a Negro, a Harlemite, an artist—
a trinity that stinks the ermine robes
of the class-conscious seraphs?
Since a headhunter lets his conscience be his guide,
I'm afraid of the blade that directs water to the bucket.

I remember the Gaya Bar on Rue Duphot—Jean
Wiener at the piano; Vance Lowry on the saxophone—
with the Stravinsky of *L'Histoire du Soldat*
and the Milhaud of *La Création du Monde*
and the Ravel of *L'Enfant et les Sortilèges;*
but I did not come home by the weeping cross:
I tried to poise that seesaw between *want* and *have*.

To explain the crossruff,
Harlem used the fig leaf
of Black Orchid,
alias the forbidden wine of Sura 78,
instead of the Rosetta stone.

The Harlem Symphony Orchestra
never, *never* cried:
"Bravo, bravo, Maestro!
Viva! Viva! il grande Mister Starks!"
Yet I deserve no pauper's grave
in a churchyard,
for,
the premiere of the *Black Orchid Suite*—
sunrise on the summit
between
sunset and sunset—
will forever stir my dust and bones
like the strains of *Ecco la marchia*
in the veins of a Mozartian.

Hideho Heights

Plato's bias will not banish,
from his Republic,
the poet laureate of Lenox Avenue—
for he is a man square as the x in Dixie,
in just the right place,
at just the right time,
with just the right thing.

I remember his credo versified at
the Market Place Gallery:
"A work of art is a two-way street,
not a dead end,
where an artist and a hipster meet.
The form and content in a picture or a song
should blend like the vowels in a dipthong.
Since this is the means and end in a design,
do I have to moan again,
'Amen'?"

He had the damp-dry eyes of the tragic-comic,
but his humor and pride were feathers
that guised the crissum of a mockingbird.

He said:
"Content is a substance beneath the bark.
Unless a craftsman
is on horseback to lark
a hedge, does he select a piece of wood
(for his artifact)
that is not good?"

To the black bourgeoisie,
Hideho was a crab louse
in the pubic region of Afroamerica.

How did he take it, O Harlem?
Like a fat leaf
about the kidney of a hog.

Dr. Igor Shears

A Jonah crab,
Igor Shears frequented deep water:
a patron of the Arts and a disciple of Walton,
he used to hustle me off to the Florida Keys
after the reneging rigmarole and *rigor caloris* of a season
with the Harlem Symphony Orchestra;
yet, the man inside was an enigma to me—a phrase
(the dove of the distant terebinths)
in the title of a Psalm.

Ma'am Shears

Her character was a cliché in the *Book of Homilies;*
and *what she was* was as legible
as a Spencerian address
in the window of an envelope.

Crazy Cain

In his tradition ran an Eliotic vein of surrender:
a bass rhythm,
florid figurations
—primitive, percussive, often contrary to the bass—
persisted in his style;
so I had to fire him from the Harlem Symphony Orchestra,
in spite of Mrs. Guy Delaporte's vase of tears.
His Negro tradition bitched the night
an Irish field hand raped a Mandingo woman in
an Alabama cottonfield.

The hybrid chattel
with a taint from Blarney
was Cain's great-grandfather:
the noxious tinge
mixed with the blues in his fingers
and the dialect in his veins.

History is a book of seven seals
from no Isle of Patmos;
but a Zulu Club Wit discovered
it was a felony to teach
a black boy his ABC's when
a whale ship was
the Harvard of
a white cabin boy.

Crazy Cain
was as ignorant of his people's past
as Charicleia in *Ethiopica*,
and the only calculus
the descendant of the hybrid chattel had
was in his bladder.
He knew
. . . yet . . .
he knew
that he was the bastard son
of Black Orchid
and
Mr. Guy Delaporte III,
but his knowing fell short of the *Poudres de Succession*.

Doctor Obi Nkomo

His psyche was a half-breed,
a bastard of Barbarus and Cultura;
and the twain shall never meet
on the D-Day dreaded by the Scholar-Gypsy.
Young Nkomo followed the Christ of the African Veld
to the Statue of Liberty,
to Wall Street,
and to Mr. Morgan's Thirteen Galleries of Art
that housed his Byzantine enamels and ivories,
his Renaissance bronzes and marbles,
his French porcelains and paintings
from the fabled Fragonard room.

There the Passion Oratorio of the odyssey stopped
like fermentation checked
by alcohol
in the must of grapes.

Dr. Shears said at a Zulu Club talk-around:
"Obi Nkomo, you are
a St. John who envisions
humanity as a thick mass of bees
with hairs on their legs—
by which they carry the collected pollen
to a collective hive."

In the gale of guffaws Obi
Nkomo's head was erect like the habit of the pagoda tree.

Then he laughed
at himself and laughed at them.
To Dr. Shears, he confided gravely:
"Thou art not the first bridegroom disillusioned by
the darling materialism of the westering star.
She butterflied the bowels of Walt Whitman.
Bedded in the Democratic Vista Inn,
the Good Gray Poet discovered
the materialism of the West was a steatopygous Jezebel
with falsies on her buttocks."

Hideho Heights
downed his *Zulu Chief* in a gulp,
palmed his chin, and said:
"As my ante in the jack pot, I'd say
Obi Nkomo is a St. John who envisions
a brush turkey that makes
a mound of the Old World's decaying vegetables
to generate heat and hatch the eggs of the New."

The aged Africanist looked up surmisingly,
his gaze leveled at Hideho Heights
as straight as the zone axis of a crystal.
"Only an Aristotelian metaphorist,"
he said,
"could conjure up an image like *that!*"

The bouquet was the geometer's horn angle
to me; but the way the Zulu Club Wits
waxed stiller than tissues in paraffin
magicked the nosegay into the cat's pajamas.

The Curator

The Harlem Gallery
. . . the creek that connects the island and the mainland . . .
. . . a *q* in Old Anglo-Saxon . . .
. . . an oasis in the Danakil Desert . . .
. . . and the mascara of dusky middlebrow matrons . . .
became the beccafico that excited the top hats,
the butt that inebriated the Zulu Club Wits,
and the butte that pinked many a butt.

The species itself is strange
in the hand or in the bush,
for wings are found
only on the chosen
and feathers grow only in distinct areas;
a fortiori,
The Curator of this variegated aviary on
Black Manhattan
emerged as a *strange* bird—
a jacobin of horny, reversed epidermal outgrowths.

Sometimes
the Harlem Gallery
was in bad odor; however—
it was not the smell of dead ideas
unembalmed and unburied.

Guy Delaporte solemnized: "I love—God knows I *love*
pictures!"
The Curator groaned: "So does Ike, the painter—except,
of course,
the moderns that give Nikita, the Art critic, a churn of a
bellyache."

· 119 ·

The brass-check *Harlem Tattler*
volleyed its barbs of bunkum
at the connoisseur; but

The Curator
stood out
in the
Death's Jest-Book of Harlem like
the Minerva with the Police Gazette Belt
catching a twenty-four-
pound, round
solid missile fired from a cannon
thirty feet away.

Everytime Guy Delaporte III farts—
the phenomenon is headlined in the Negro press;
so, interviewed, he said: "The Curator is a Greenland shark
feeding on the carcass of a whale
in spite of stabs in the head!"

SO—the moods of The Curator
varied from the white stripe over
the goshawk's eye
to the dark patch
back of it.

I remember, oh, I remember how
irony trumped his coat card,
the prodigy
Richard Fairfax.

When the young artist
knuckled under as a gigolo
of Black and Tan Skin-Whiteners, Inc.,
The Curator grew angrier than Cellini, *when,*
behind a hedge,
he saw young Luigi Pulci in the arms
of the whore Pantasilea.

Doctor Nkomo caricatured
The Curator as a dusky
Francis I of France
with an everlasting cartel of defiance;
but among the Harlem middlebrows
there was not even a side-show Richelieu
to check a duel of end men with pasteboard razors!

The Harlem Gallery his *Malakoff,*
I can imagine his saying to
anyone
who advised him to leave,
"J'y suis, j'y reste."

I used to say if I knew the differences between
The Curator and Doctor Nkomo,
· I'd know the ebb and flow of tides of color.

Then I made the discovery
in the dawn hours
after the Zulu Club habitués
had floundered into Lenox Avenue.

The janitor—an incognito
ex-chaplain from Alabama Christian College—
performed the ritual of cap and bells
with mop and broom;
the ex-Freedom Rider had explained earlier:
"Gentlemen,
when any Old Ship of State
rams a reef of history,
the passengers
as well as the sailors
are involved."

We chewed this quid a second time,
for Black Boy often adds
the dimension of ethnic irony
to Empson's classic seven.

While The Curator sipped his cream
and Doctor Nkomo swigged his homogenized milk,
I tried to gin the secret of
the mutuality of minds
that moved independently of each other—
like the eyeballs of a chameleon.

"Why cream, O Nestor, instead of milk?"
Doctor Nkomo's guileless question
was a whore at the altar in a virgin's wedding gown.

The Curator's reply
had Taine's smell of the laboratory.

Whether that's good or bad
depends on one's stance,
upstage—or—downstage.

As The Curator spoke, there was no
mule-deer's-tail contrast
of white and black in the way he said it:
"I remain a lactoscopist
fascinated by
the opacity of cream,
the dusk of human nature,
'the light-between' of the modernistic."

Doctor Nkomo's snort
was a Cape buffalo's.
"You brainwashed, whitewashed son
of bastard Afroamerica!"
The Curator grinned
his Solomonic grin,
for the nettle words were stingless like
a mosquito bee.
As a Bach fugue piles up rhythms,
the Africanist heaped his epithets:
"Garbed in the purple of metaphors,
the Nordic's theory of the cream separator
is still a stinking skeleton!"

"Since cream rises to the top," said The Curator,
"blame Omniscience—
not me."
The Curator liked to dangle Socratic bait!

"Perhaps Omniscience deigns to colorbreed."
Lips parted like the bivalves of an oyster,
the ex-chaplain and neo-janitor
put his mop aside and sideslipped toward our table,
his eyes sweethearting a chair.

I needed a shock absorber as
Doctor Nkomo,
with Lionelbarrymorean gestures,
Homerized a spiritual:

*"Sit down, servant, please sit down,
sit down, servant, please sit down,
sit down, servant, please sit down,
you done earned your heavenly crown!"*

Our crowing laughs and clapping palms
had the scaling motion of
clay pigeons from a trap of the *fin de siècle*.

His D.D. robe
(but not his affidavit of integrity)
in a Harlem pawn shop,
the ex-chaplain continued mockingly:
"Gentlemen,
according to the *Anglo-Saxon Chronicle*,
so potent is one drop of African blood
that, in the zero of a second, it
can turn the whitest Nordic into a Negro.

"Gentlemen,
perhaps there is a symbolism
—a manna for the darker peoples—
in the rich opacity of cream
and the poor whiteness of skim milk."

Among such eggheads,
I was glad that I had on
my thick-lensed glasses,
as the sex image of a Mary of Magdala
with kinky hair and a cream complexion
hula-hulaed across my mind.

(Will mortals ever become mind readers? God forbid!)

The Afroamerican's features of *A Man called White*
paled like the fatty sheath of nerve fibers,
and the African's jet eyes grew
as soft as the fin of a mirror carp.

"Between the ass and the womb of two eras,"
said The Curator, gloomily,
"*taste* the milk of the skimmed
and *sip* the cream of the skimmers."

To the old Africanist,
this eclipse of faith felt and seen in *mens agitat molem*
had the bitterness of dried cones of hops—
without
malt liquors.

"Mens sibi conscia recti,"
said Doctor Nkomo
—definitively—
"is not a hollow man who dares not peddle
the homogenized milk of multiculture,
in dead ends and on boulevards,
in green pastures and across valleys of dry bones."

Whatever the effect of this altitude,
it was hidden behind The Curator's mask—
like a tailor bird's nest
behind stitched-together leaves.

Nothing is so desolating
as a deserted night club
with Is seated in the chair of Is Not—
the skull of a way of life that faces the crack of doom
with wine and wit and wiggle.

The Curator and Doctor Nkomo
sat staring into space,
united like the siphons of a Dosinia—
the oddest hipsters on the new horizon of Harlem,
odder
(by odds)
than that
cabala of a funeral parlor
in Cuernavaca,
Mexico
. . . called . . .
"Quo Vadis."

Mrs. Guy Delaporte III

Her temperament
was the mercurial pendulum
of a Riefler's clock—
and her
bent the bias
of a river on a map.
Cultivated in the greenhouse
of an Electra complex,
she was a delicate plant exposed
to the arctic circle of the black Sodom;
so her leaflets closed tight
and her leafstalk drooped in fits of relapsing fever.

John Laugart

Daumier, blind and paralytic, gave up the ghost
in Paris;
Laugart reviled but pot-valiant, a stiletto sucked his veins
dry
in Harlem:
each a bowl from the Potter's wheel
the State buried in a potter's field,
like the one the chief priests bought
in Jerusalem—
for thirty pieces of silver:
his road was a hogback unfit for even
a half-blind black son of Hagar.
The ominous rattle of his bones will never disturb
the tryst of graveyard lovers.

Big Mama

Her conscience was a little clay ball,
　　baked hard and oiled,
　　ready for the use of any hand;
　　and her past was a hidden vanity box in which
she had stashed away many coups of the fleshpots.
　　When I was a piano-plunker
　　in her Niflheim speakeasy,
　　I heard her say once to Dutch Schultz:
　　"I was born in Rat Alley.
　　I live on Fox Avenue.
　　I shall die in Buzzard Street."
　　I remember the kingbolt guffawed
　　and slapped her elephantine buttocks
and planted a century note in her bediamonded claw
　　and said in a funereal voice:
　　"Big Mama,
　　you and I were born under the same star."
　　I remember the faces of his fingermen—
　　yellowish gray and hard as tala.

One of the Derbies leaned on the upright—winked,
and nodded at the keyboard as I took a swig of bootleg.
　　Fishing for an apposite figure,
　　my fingers wandered and wondered
　　up and down, up and down,
　　in a corny polka style
reminiscent of Kid Ory's trombone in *Sweet Little Papa*.

"I wanted to be a Caruso," the Derby mused.
(Self-pity is conspicuous consumption of the soul.)
I pitched him a ball with a crazy break. "Sidetracked?"
"Hell, no!" he groused. "Derailed."
His laugh was as hollow as *La fin de Babylon*.
"It happens sometimes in the *best* families, Mister."
His chin was the jut of the *Agamemnon's* prow.
"And any time in the *worst!*" he sharped.

Like all 100-p.c. Negroes,
I knew a white skin was the open
sesame to SUCCESS—
the touchstone of
Freedom, Justice, Equality.
Hadn't a white poet said when they cut off his leg,
"I am the master of my fate . . ."?
So, the class struggle was a myth
manufactured in Moscow by the Red White Russians.
I could see why a 100-p.c. white man said, "Goddamn 'em!"

The guy's getting soft,
I thought.
In the twilight world,
dissonance is white and yellow
directed by a skeleton whose baton is a scythe.

As I explored the theme phrase,
a new rhythm and melody vistaed before me:
the tones feathered into chords
and leafed and interlaced
in fluxing chromatic figures.

Perhaps I'd had too many swigs of bootleg!
Anyway, the cigarette smoke
caricatured not only the Derby but my vision of
the African who had dramatized integration as
the notes of white keys and black keys
blended in the majestic *tempo di marcia* of Man.

The speakeasy was as quiet as
a medicine-subdued pulse;
and Big Mama's face was a
shiny slab of serpentine
marble as Dutch Schultz, a jovial Friar Tuck,
bulged at my elbow.
"If you ever need a job," he said,
"remember my elevator."
But it was the Derby that
became a Socratic gadfly:
"What is it, Mister?"
(Put the notes on the staff, Black Boy!)
My answer was a suspended tone
as I recaptured the African's ethnic metaphors
of the narrow upper keys and the broad lower keys.
I looked up at those faces in man's twilight zone:
staves of mutilated notes on
the music rack of the Great White World's concert grand.
Then I magicked an arpeggio of syncopated colors
(my left hand, like Fats', suggesting a bass fiddle)
and said with a flourish, *"Rhapsody in Black and White."*
It was the feel
for a tangent to a curve with a straightedge—
or the image of Bast in a royal stable.

No ear trumpet was needed:
the theme of
Rhapsody in Black and White
was an answer to
Tin Pan Alley's blues classic—
or, maybe, it was only a buteo
seeking peaks in the breeding season—
a butcherbird
impaling its prey on thorns.
I was—like every other artist—
an incorrigible gambler.
The stakes?
Caesar or God!
(Put the notes on the staff, Black Boy!)
As Caesar seized Alesia,
I grabbed
the bottle of bootleg,
drained it to its vilest dregs,
and stumbled toward the exit guarded by
that Cerebean ex-pug,
Tiger Tyler,
who had fought the Boston Tar Baby
on the apex of the soapy pyramid
when the cauliflowered Master was
Jack Johnson's
Banquo's ghost
of the squared circle—
merry-andrewed.

A man is juice (said Doctor Nkomo) pressed from the
apples of life—juice made hard or sweet or bitter.

Like a biased ball on a level plat of green,
I bowled past the Derby.
Again he stammered, *"What—is it?"*
Big Mama's mind was a rear-vision mirror,
since she said, "You wouldn't understand."
With the hubris of a Hippias,
Dutch Schultz challenged,
"Is my stuff that bad?"
(Put the notes on the staff, Black Boy!)

A Magdalene loitered near the subway.
She had the olive complexion of a Brahui
and the smoldering eyes of lighted coals in ashes.
Out of the shadows came a handsome yellow man.
As the cheap melodrama unfolded,
I felt sorry for the unsuspecting woman.
About to pass, I said, "Hello, Officer!"
The surprise of the Vice Squad cop was Macbeth's
when he discovered Macduff
had been ripped alive from his mother's womb.

In the Abraham's bosom of Pisano's café,
I ordered a Dixie Mixie. Later, Pisano whispered,
"I have *The Protocols of the Wise Men of Zion.*"
Brows hedged, he leaned between
the beetle and the block.
"Signor," I said, "that corpse stank a thousand years ago."
As if from the upward pressure of a buoy,
the hedge brows lifted.
Then came the sockdolager, "The Antichrist!"
(Put the notes on the staff, Black Boy!)

PHI

Harlem Vignettes read,
I felt I should make
(like Hideho)
a second Harlem marriage bed—
take
(like Hideho)
the Daughter of the Wine to Spouse:
sudden sunlight
blinds the mole;
sudden darkness,
the field mouse.

That night in the Zulu Club
the man who had already willed to die
had seen in me
the failure of nerve
Harlem would never see—
the charact in the African
that made
him the better man.

Vanity,
gas
and art
vapor away in Harlem:
I thought the verse of Mister Starks
a smokestack
contrived without book, to prevent
the escape of sparks.

I've walked many a Walk
in Harlem—
seen it crumble away.
I've heard many a Say—
deciphered
its epitaph on its natal day:

the birth-after-the-father-is-buried
Harlem Vignettes
will doubtless fetch
no white laurel of joys,
no black crepe of regrets.

Lice, like men, desert a corpse.
Yet my conscience,
when it has a tittle to do,
feels pricks of *Harlem Vignettes*—like a
horse's foot
in nailing on a shoe.

After the performance of the Angelus Funeral Home,
sophists of the black-and-tan,
anointers of the black-and-blue,
cool, man, cool as bubbles at the spirit level—
entered again the Dollar Cockpit of Custom and the Van;
so, sometimes,
I join the great laughers
. . . Gogol . . .
. . . Dickens . . .
. . . Rabelais . .
in the black world of white Manhattan.

Black Boy,
listen! Let no man lie
in the throat about the Noble Savage
of the Trek of Tears
and the Middle Passage.

Beneath the sun
as he clutched the bars of a barracoon,
beneath the moon
of a blind and deaf-mute Sky,
my forebears heard a Cameroon
chief, in the language of the King James Bible, cry,
"O Absalom, my son, my son!"

Solons of Jim Crow,
sages as far as the beard,
cipher and cipher and cipher—
and ask, "What is a Negro?"
Again,
O bastard son
of occult identity,
we who are we
on the boards of the *Théâtre Vie*
face the prongs of Horton's fork
and the horns of Rimbaud's Ogaden.
I've seen the isms of phile and phobe yeast-
bitten as they brewed their malt and hops
for a Barmecide feast.

His motive burled
like tufted wool,
Shadrach Martial Kilroy
set free the bull
of a fixed idea in the china shop of the Zulu Club:
"O *Homo Caucasicus,*
a specter haunts the Great White World—
the specter of *Homo Aethiopicus,*
the pigmented Banquo's ghost!"

Since he put no Judas in his mouth
to steal away his brains,
Doctor Nkomo said: "As regards the Negro, you
are a people in whose veins
poly-breeds
and
plural strains
mingle and run—
an Albert Rider of many schools,
and *none.*
Since only the unpigmented wear
a cravat
of civil rights,
the vanity
of the Iscariots of
the Republic pancakes
your star of destiny flat
as a depressed appetite; so,
your black dog trapped like an ex-sewage rat,
you go
from the dead end of this to the dead end of that."

The bravado of Mr. Kilroy refused
to let the millstones
grind the grain
of his Race Pride; so he bellylaughed:
"In the five great zones,
the quickie-work *Negro* varies like a Siamese noun
with five different meanings in five different tones."

Doctor Nkomo said:
"Let us not rattle the dry bones of statistics—
like the dead-
alive in an academic waste land.
As man to man,
should you and I grovel in dust and ashes because
of *what* I think of you or *what* you think of me?
God damns that tit for tat!
Even Mr. K would say
every *sookin sin* must find—like Jacob—
his stone, *his* ladder, *his* seed of destiny."

Where are the gray eyes and blond ears?
Ay—Black Boy—there's the rub!
Mr. Kilroy's curiosity
swiveled about the Zulu Club.
No ofays indoors,
he became intimate,
perforce,
like a Puritan in
an illicit intercourse:

"Blackamoors,
this kinky-head, Obi Nkomo, is *rough!*"
Hideho Heights corrected him,
"I say, as the People's Poet, this cat is *tough!*"

The poet, later, gave me a mystifying nod
and began his dubious trek to the bar,
on wobbly legs that reminded me of the
shimmying, shilly-shally
wheels of a car.

He right-angled his shoulders,
shook his senses clear of the devil-may-care
smog of *Zulu Chief;* then his poet's conscience became
an upright like a post in a ladderback chair.

I waited.
"Of course, you've read
Dolph Peeler's *Ode to the South.*"
I nodded,
"His symbol of the pig in the boa's coils wasn't bad."
He wiped his mouth.
"Defeatist!"
He pawed his head.
"That bunkum session on the Negro,"
he said,
"has sparked an inspiration."
I thought,
*The old stock mare of poets,
living and dead.*

I was caught up in
the strident hum
of a
whirling Ferris wheel.
"Yo—ho—ho and a bottle of rum!"
he exclaimed.
"The Centennial of the Emancipation Proclamation,
Ye Muses!
As the People's Poet,
I shall Homerize a theme that will rock the Nation!
And every damned Un-American will know it!"

My blab-blab-blab
was a dip to free his sheep
of vermin and scab:
"You poets come too soon or too late,
Hideho Heights,
with too little,
to save the Old Ship of State.
Remember to remember
a tribal anthem
is the yankee-doodle-diddle of a tittle."

To Hideho Heights,
at that moment in the throe
of creation,
I was a half-white egghead with maggots on the brain.
I ate my crow,
for the unconscious of the artist
cannot say to itself *No*.

My clichés at the bar
were bones in the maw of the tomb,
but the idea in Hideho's brain
was an embryo,
head down,
in the
womb!

"What's the big idea?"
I razzed.
Jerked out of his trance,
he put his fists on guard,
jazzed,
feinted,
in the grotesquerie of a boxer's stance.

I waited.
"This is . . . IT—
Curator.
Follow the spoor of the symbols—if you have the wit!
Strange but true is the story
of the sea-turtle and the shark—
the instinctive drive of the weak to survive
in the oceanic dark.
Driven,
riven
by hunger
from abyss to shoal,
sometimes the shark swallows
the sea-turtle whole.

"The sly reptilian marine
withdraws,
into the shell
of his undersea craft,
his leathery head and the rapacious claws
that can rip
a rhinoceros' hide
or strip
a crocodile to fare-thee-well;
now,
inside the shark,
the sea-turtle begins the churning seesaws
of his descent into pelagic hell;
then . . . *then,*
with ravenous jaws
that can cut sheet steel scrap,
the sea-turtle gnaws
. . . and gnaws . . . and gnaws . . .
his way in a way that appalls—
his way to freedom,
beyond the vomiting dark,
beyond the stomach walls
of the shark."

I was conscious of the Zulu Club Wits
tied neck and heels by a poetic analogy—
conscious of the poet's posture,
an S-shaped gut on the stool beside me;
but I knew his helm was in line with his keel
as an artist's helm should be.

If fiction is stranger than truth,
I must have been on a bender
when my old T-total crony,
the Jamaican bartender—
who had eased up
to hear Hideho's hot
tale—overhastily downed a double shot
of *Zulu Chief,*
as if it were two per cent in a cider cup.

Above the fluke of a nose,
under a shag of brows,
glowed hard coal embers
that had borne witness to the troubled repose
of crucified Junes and Decembers;
and from the cavern of a mouth
came words quiet and englished and dark:
"God knows, Hideho, you got the low-down
on the black turtle and the white shark
in the Deep South."
Then,
describing a pectoral girdle,
his lower lip curled,
and he blurted—like an orgasm:
"And perhaps in many a South of the Great White World!"
He fumed, he sweated, he paced behind the bar.
"I too hate Peeler's pig in the boa's coils!
I was in the bomb-hell at Dunkirk. I was a British tar.
In Parliament, *white* Churchill quoted one day,
'If we must die, let us not die like hogs . . .'
The words of a poet, my compatriot—*black* Claude McKay."

O Zulu Club Wits,
a tavern is the sunshiniest place
in the black ghetto—
a now paradise
free from
creditors and saviors,
blowflies and lice:
it *is*
a city of refuge,
for those who have fallen from grace,
for those who are tired of the rat-race
(the everlasting—*On your mark! Get set! Go!*)
in the Land of the Gray Flannel Suit
and the Home of the Portfolio!

Never before,
in the tavern of the Zulu Club,
nor in the cabaret downstairs,
had Hideho left the cellar door
of his art ajar, with a Promethean gesture,
so we could get our penny's worth:
"Everybody has a private gallery.
In mine is a whore giving birth
to a pimp's son, Curator, on a filthy quilt.
(In travail a woman shows no sign of guilt.)
I was lucky to get the candid shots
through cracks in the ruins called a flat.
I was a kid
. . . then . . .
with the unbridled intelligence of
Professor Marotelli's cat.

"Maybe, yes, maybe,
an artist's travail is like
a woman's; and her baby is like
a poem, a picture, a symphony—
an issue of the *élan vital* in sweat and blood,
born on a brazen
sea and swaddled
on a raft of life and shaped like a question mark.
If we split hairs, there is no midwife
at one's beck and call
in the Kingdom of Poetry;
and a pregnancy
with its hopes and fears
may encompass many tomorrows,
while the travail may ebb and flow for years.
Then, too,
consider the abortions
of the *howl-howl-with-the-combo* quacks;
the little Eddie Jests and Shortfellows who use no rubbers
when copulating with muses on the wrong side of the tracks;
the new-born sun-god babes snatched
from cradles on the sly;
the bigname poets,
sober or high,
who abandon the little
hybrid bastards of their youth
without
saying,
'Good-by!' "

CHI

Despite his caricatures
of poets and poetasters,
Hideho's joy was Hasidic
among the lives and works of the Masters—
old and new.
He himself was a sort of aged Istanbul
with a young Beyoglu.

He didn't know
I knew
about the split identity
of the People's Poet—
the bifacial nature of his poetry:
the racial ballad in the public domain
and the private poem in the modern vein.

I had overheard the poet say:
"Reverend Eli, in a foxhole
with the banzai in my ears,
one day
I collapsed from battle fatigue.
You know why?
Since I was unable to dig
the immortality of John Doe,
fears
(not Hamlet's . . . not Simon Legree's),
my fears
of oblivion made me realistic:
with no poems of Hideho's in World Lit—
he'd be a statistic!"

Poor Boy Blue,
the Great White World
and the Black Bourgeoisie
have shoved the Negro artist into
the white and not-white dichotomy,
the Afroamerican dilemma in the Arts—
the dialectic of
to be or not to be
a Negro.

From the grandeur that was dusky Rome,
one night I brought Hideho home,
dead drunk,
in a Zulu Club taxicab.
As he lay on the sofa,
ashy-black like a stiff on a slab
in a Harlem morgue,
I chanced to see,
in the modern idiom,
a poem called *E. & O. E.*
(A sort of Pasternakian secrecy, I thought.)
I was again the kid startled by the kettledrum
on the withers of a cavalry horse.
(Cry havoc, Poor Boy Blue.)
That he had been
a bistro habitué,
an expatriate poet of the Black Venus
in the Age of Whoopee—
Clotho had kept hid until then.

For the skeptic
on Lenox Avenue,
for the goof
on Peach-tree Street—
here was the eyesight proof
that the Color Line, as well as the Party Line,
splits an artist's identity
like the vertical which
Omar's *Is* and *Is-not* cannot define.
The face
of no man escapes the common gable roof
of this time, nor the lights and shadows in the design
of that place.

Why should a man,
in an age of anesthesiology,
seek relief
in the bark of the toothache tree?
Yet,
depressed like ondoyant glass,
Hideho Heights,
the *Coeur de Lion* of the Negro mass,
in *E. & O. E.* rationalized:
"Why place an empty pail
before a well
of dry bones?
Why go to Nineveh to tell
the ailing that they ail?
Why lose a golden fleece
to gain a holy grail?"

The Hideho Heights that Afroamerican Freedom, Inc.,
glorified
had recognition marks—plain
like the white tail of an antelope;
in the subterrane
of this poem, however,
the protagonist aped the dubiety
of a wet cake of soap.

. . .

Yet,
in front of the ramshackle
theatre that had graduated into
the Ethiopian Tabernacle,
like sandstone into gneiss,
Hideho had left "Bishop" Gladstone Coffin
tongue-tied as a puking slop-bowl gobbler with a con head
that had a Napoleonic forelock, but a naked monkey ass
behind.
Jailed for disturbing the peace, he had said
later, to the liquored-up Zulu Club Wits:
"A man's conscience is home-bred.
To see an artist or a leader do
Uncle Tom's asinine splits
is an ask-your-mama shame!"
The Jamaican bartender had staked off his claim:
"The drinks are on the house, Poet Defender!"
A sportsman with ruffed grouse
on the wing over dogs, the poet had continued:
"Integrity is an underpin—
the marble lions that support
the alabaster fountain in
the Alhambra."

. . .

In the poem, *E. & O. E.,*
The poet's mind kept shuttling between
the sphinx of Yesterday and the enigma of Today,
like the specter of Amphion in Thebes
'twixt fragments of requiems and stones of decay.

Time!
Time?
The poet's *bête noire*, I thought.
We everyday mortals
wrought
on the cis-threshold of the sublime
are concerned with *timing*,
not with *time*.

I remembered the wisdom
of a grand duchess of the burlesque shows,
whose G-string gave repose
to no man's imagination.
"It's all in the timing,"
said Rose La Rose,
Mister Minsky's tigress in heat.
Just as sound,
not spelling,
is the white magic of rhyming
in the poet's feat,
the timing
of a parson's spiel,
of an H-bomb,
of a golfer's swing,
of a curator's budget—
makes the gallery ring!

I
(conscious of my Judas role)
jumped
when Hideho's foot
plumped
against the floor;
but in a second flat
the broken-down flat vibrated again with the snore
of a mine pump's suction hole.

I cudgeled again the eyesight proof:
"I am no ape
of Benares. I have won
no Monthyon
prize. Though I
have cut a G clef and a belletristic S,
naked on
roller skates in Butte Montmartre,
sweated palm to palm
to the down beats of
the tom-tom,
in Sorgue's studio
with the Black Venus,
and, a leaning question mark upon
a blue white metal bar, drunk piccolo
with Salmon, Apollinaire,
MacOrlan, and Picasso—
yet, out of square,
I have not said,
'Hippoclides doesn't care.'"

My unbelief
as I climbed the Peak of Teneriffe
in the poem
... grew ...
indistinct
... grew ...
invisible,
like the veins between the stem and margin of a leaf:

"Beneath
the albatross,
the skull-and-bones,
the Skull and Cross,
the Seven Sins Dialectical,
I do not shake
the Wailing Wall
of Earth—
nor quake
the Gethsemane
of Sea—
nor tear
the Big Top
of Sky
with Lear's prayer,
or Barabas' curse,
or Job's cry!"

PSI

Black Boy,
let me get up from the white man's Table of Fifty Sounds
in the kitchen; let me gather the crumbs and cracklings
of this autobio-fragment,
before the curtain with the skull and bones descends.

Many a *t* in the ms.
I've left without a cross,
many an *i* without a dot.
A dusky Lot
with a third degree and a second wind and a seventh turn
of pitch-and-toss,
my psyche escaped the Sodom of Gylt
and the Big White Boss.

Black Boy,
you stand before your heritage,
naked and agape;
cheated like a mockingbird
pecking at a Zuexian grape,
pressed like an awl to do
duty as a screw-
driver, you
ask the American Dilemma in you:
"If the trying plane
of Demos fail,
what will the trowel
of Uncle Tom avail?"

Black Boy,
in this race, at this time, in this place,
to be a Negro artist is to be
a flower of the gods, whose growth
is dwarfed at an early stage—
a Brazilian owl moth,
a giant among his own in an acreage
dark with the darkman's designs,
where the milieu moves back downward like the sloth.

Black Boy,
true—you
have not
dined and wined
(*ignoti nulla cupido*)
in the El Dorado of aeried Art,
for unreasoned reasons;
and your artists, not so lucky as the Buteo,
find themselves without a
skyscape sanctuary
in the
season of seasons:
in contempt of the contemptible,
refuse the herb of grace, the rue
of Job's comforter;
take no
lie-tea in lieu
of Broken Orange Pekoe.
Doctor Nkomo said: "*What* is he who smacks
his lips when dewrot eats away the golden grain
of self-respect exposed like flax
to the rigors of sun and rain?"

Black Boy,
every culture,
every caste,
every people,
every class,
facing the barbarians
with lips hubris-curled,
believes its death rattle omens
the *Dies Irae* of the world.

Black Boy,
summon Boas and Dephino,
Blumenbach and Koelreuter,
from their posts
around the gravestone of Bilbo,
who, with cancer in his mouth,
orated until he quaked the magnolias of the South,
while the pocketbooks of his weeping black serfs
shriveled in the drouth;
summon the ghosts
of scholars with rams' horns from Jericho
and facies in letters from Jerusalem,
so
we may ask them:
"What is a Negro?"

Black Boy,
what's in a people's name that wries the brain
like the neck of a barley bird?
Can sounding brass create
an ecotype with a word?

Black Boy,
beware of the thin-bladed mercy
stroke, for one drop of Negro blood
(V. *The Black Act of the F. F. V.*)
opens the flood-
gates of the rising tide of color
and jettisons
the D. A. R. in the Heraclitean flux
with Uncle Tom and
Crispus Attucks.
The Black Belt White,
painstaking as a bedbug in
a tenant farmer's truckle bed,
rabbit-punched old Darrow
because
he quoted Darwin's sacred laws
(instead of the Lord God Almighty's)
and gabbled that the Catarrhine ape
(the C from a Canada goose nobody knows)
appears,
after X's of years,
in the vestigial shape
of the Nordic's thin lips, his aquiline nose,
his straight hair,
orangutanish on legs and chest and head.
Doctor Nkomo, a votary of touch-and-go,
who can stand the gaff
of Negrophobes and, like Aramis,
parry a thrust with a laugh,
said:

"In spite of the pig in the python's coils,
in spite of Blake's lamb in the jaws of the tiger,
Nature is kind, even in the raw: she toils
. . . aeons and aeons and aeons . . .
gives the African a fleecy canopy
to protect the seven faculties of the brain
from the burning convex lens of the sun;
she foils
whiteness
(without disdain)
to bless the African
(as Herodotus marvels)
with the birthright of a burnt skin for work or fun;
she roils
the Aryan
(as his eye and ear repose)
to give the African an accommodation nose
that cools the drying-up air;
she entangles the epidermis in broils
that keep the African's body free from lice-infested hair.
As man to man,
the Logos is
Nature is on the square
with the African.
If a black man circles the rim
of the Great White World, he will find
(even if Adamness has made him half blind)
the bitter waters of Marah *and*
the fresh fountains of Elim."

Although his transition
was a far cry
from Shakespeare to Sardou,
the old Africanist's byplay gave
no soothing feverfew
to the Dogs in the Zulu Club;
said he:
"A Hardyesque artistry
of circumstance
divides the Whites and Blacks in life,
like the bodies of the dead
eaten by vultures
in a Tower of Silence.
Let, then, the man with a maggot in his head
lean . . . lean . . . lean
on race or caste or class,
for the wingless worms of blowflies shall grub,
dry and clean,
the stinking skeletons of these,
when the face of the macabre weather-
cock turns to the torrid wind of misanthropy;
and later their bones shall be swept together
(like the Parsees')
in the Sepulchre of Anonymity."
A Zulu Wit cleared away his unsunned
mood with dark laughter;
but I sensed the thoughts of Doctor Nkomo
pacing nervously to and fro
like Asscher's, after
he'd cleaved the giant Cullinan Diamond.

Black Boy,
the vineyard is the fittest place
in which to booze (with Omar) and study
soil and time and integrity—
the telltale triad of grape and race.

Palates that can read the italics
of *salt* and *sugar* know
a grapevine
transplanted from Bordeaux
to Pleasant Valley
cannot give grapes that make a Bordeaux wine.

Like the sons of the lone mother of dead empires,
who boasted their ancestors,
page after page—
wines are peacocky
in their vintage and their age,
disdaining the dark ways of those engaging
in the profits
of chemical aging.
When the bluebirds sing
their perennial anthem
a capriccio, in the Spring,
the sap begins to move up the stem
of the vine, and the wine in the bed of the deep
cask stirs in its winter sleep.
Its bouquet
comes with the years, dry or wet;
so the connoisseurs say:
"The history of the wine
is repeated by the vine."

Black Boy,
beware of wine labels,
for the Republic does not guarantee
what the phrase "Château Bottled" means—
the estate, the proprietor, the quality.
This ignominy will baffle you, Black Boy,
because the white man's law
has raked your butt many a time
with fang and claw.
Beware of the waiter who wraps
a napkin around your Clos Saint Thierry,
if Chance takes you into high-hat places
open to all creeds and races
born to be or not to be.
Beware of the pop
of a champagne cork:
like the flatted fifth and octave jump in Bebop,
it is theatrical
in Vicksburg or New York.
Beware of the champagne cork
that does not swell up like your ma when she had you—*that*
comes out flat,
because the bottle of wine
is dead . . . dead
like Uncle Tom and the Jim Crow Sign.
Beware . . . yet
your dreams in the Great White World
shall be unthrottled
by pigmented and unpigmented lionhearts,
for we know *without no*
every people, by and by, produces its "Château Bottled."

White Boy,
as regards the ethnic origin
of Black Boy and me,
the *What* in Socrates' *"Tò tí?"*
is for the musk-ox habitat of anthropologists;
but there is another question,
dangerous as a moutaba tick,
secreted in the house
of every Anglo-Saxon sophist and hick:

Who is a Negro?
(I am a White in deah ole Norfolk.)
Who is a White?
(I am a Negro in little old New York.)
Since my mongrelization is invisible
and my Negroness a state of mind conjured up
by Stereotypus, I am a chameleon
on *that* side of the Mason-Dixon
that a white man's conscience
is not on.
My skin is as white
as a Roman's toga when he sought an office on the sly;
my hair is as blond
as xanthein;
my eyes are as blue
as the hawk's-eye.
At the Olympian powwow of curators,
when I revealed my Negroness,
my peers became shocked like virgins in a house
where satyrs tattooed on female thighs heralds of success.

White Boy,
counterfeit scholars have used
the newest brush-on Satinlac,
to make our ethnic identity
crystal clear for the lowest IQ
in every mansion and in every shack.
Therefore,
according to the myth that Negrophobes bequeath
to the Lost Gray Cause, since Black Boy is the color
of betel-stained teeth,
he and I
(from ocular proof
that cannot goof)
belong to races
whose dust-of-the-earth progenitors
the Lord God Almighty created
of different bloods,
in antipodal places.
However,
even the F. F. V. pate
is aware that laws defining a Negro
blackjack each other within and without a state.
The Great White World, White Boy, leaves you in a sweat
like a pitcher with three runners on the bases;
and, like Kant, you seldom get
your grammar straight—yet,
you are the wick that absorbs the oil in my lamp,
in all kinds of weather;
and we are teeth in the pitch wheel
that work together.

White Boy,
when I hear the word *Negro* defined,
why does it bring to mind
the chef, the gourmand, the belly-god,
the disease of kings, the culinary art
in alien lands, Black Mammy in a Dixie big house,
and the dietitian's chart?
Now, look at Black Boy scratch his head!
It's a stereotypic gesture of Uncle Tom,
a learned Gentleman of Color said
in his monumental tome,
The *Etiquette of the New Negro,*
which,
the publishers say,
by the way,
should be in every black man's home.

The Negro is a dish in the white man's kitchen—
a potpourri,
an ola-podrida,
a mixie-maxie,
a hotchpotch of lineal ingredients;
with UN guests at his table,
the host finds himself a Hamlet on the spot,
for, in spite of his catholic pose,
the Negro dish is a dish nobody knows:
to some . . . tasty,
like an exotic condiment—
to others . . . unsavory
and inelegant.

White Boy,
the Negro dish is a mix
like . . . and *un*like
pimiento brisque, chop suey,
eggs à la Goldenrod, and eggaroni;
tongue-and-corn casserole, mulligan stew,
baked fillets of halibut, and cheese fondue;
macaroni milanaise, egg-milk shake,
mullagatawny soup, and sour-milk cake.

Just as the Chinese lack
an ideogram for "to be,"
our lexicon has no definition
for an ethnic amalgam like Black Boy and me.

Behold a Gordian knot without
the *beau geste* of an Alexander's sword!
Water, O Modern Mariner, water, everywhere,
unfit for *vitro di trina* glass
or the old-oaken-bucket's gourd!

For dark hymens on the auction block,
the lord of the mansion knew the macabre score:
not a dog moved his tongue,
not a lamb lost a drop of blood to protect a door.
O
Xenos of Xanthos,
what midnight-to-dawn lecheries,
in cabin and big house,
produced these brown hybrids and yellow motleys?

White Boy,
Buchenwald is a melismatic song
whose single syllable is sung to blues notes
to dark wayfarers who listen for the gong
at the crack of doom along
. . . that Lonesome Road . . .
before they travel on.

A Pelagian with the *raison d'être* of a Negro,
I cannot say I have outwitted dread,
for I am conscious of the noiseless tread
of the Yazoo tiger's ball-like pads behind me
in the dark
as I trudge ahead,
up and up . . . that Lonesome Road . . . up and up.

In a Vision in a Dream,
from the frigid seaport of the proud Xanthochroid,
the good ship *Défineznegro*
sailed fine, under an unabridged moon,
to reach the archipelago
Nigeridentité.
In the Strait of Octoroon,
off black Scylla,
after the typhoon Phobos, out of the Stereotypus Sea,
had rived her hull and sail to a T,
the *Défineznegro* sank the rock
and disappeared in the abyss
(*Vanitas vanitatum!*)
of white Charybdis.

OMEGA

White Boy,
Black Boy,
you have played blackjack with Tyche,
you have shot craps with Hap;
yet, things-as-they-are in the ghetto
have sported you for a sap.
Sometimes,
a guy born in a house with the graffito
of doom lucks upon the know-how of a raccoon
that gnaws off its leg to escape from a trap.
Now, the difference between
you and me
is the little matter of
a Harvard Ph. D.
You may have a better brain—
but no Nestor taught you how
to get rid of
its ball and chain.

Those in the upper drawer give a child
the open sesame to the unknown
What and How and Why;
that's *that* which curators, as Pelagians, try
to do
in exhibitions,
when a genius gets through
with a nonpareil of art whose exegesis
exacts patience—the patience of a cow
that sucks lime from a deer
antler dropped at the dawn of the year.

Black Boy,
White Boy,
a lesser dog that diadems an eked-out butt of space
may baffle Palomar's eye;
yet, no Schaeberle thumbs his nose at the discovery
and scowls, "Good-by!"

"At the crossroads, does painting take,"
as Lhote said,
"the direction of the merchant?"
Should the artist stand on his head
in the middle of Main Street,
to get the coppers of the vulgar?
Paint an *ignis fatuus* of *nawiht*,
to win thirty pieces of silver from the elite?

Sometimes a work of art is bitter crystalline alkaloid
to be doled out
at intervals, between the laugh and flout
of an Admirable Doctor; but, if taken too much
at a time, it delivers the cocainizing punch
of a Jack Dempsey nonesuch.

Many mouths empty their waters
into the Godavari of Art—
a river that flows
across the Decan trap of the age
with its lava-scarred plateaux;
and, in the selfheal of the river,
pilgrims lave the bruises of the Rain of woes.

White Boy,
Black Boy,
the meander of a curator leads him by
the house where Illiteracy beds
with Ignorance and all her brats.
Should he
skim the milk of culture for the elite
and give the "lesser breeds"
a popular latex brand?
Should he
(to increase digestibility)
break up
the fat globules and vitamins and casein shreds?
Tonic spasms of wind and wave
assail compass and lamp in the cabined night;
but the binnacle of imagination
steers the work of art aright—
even if the craftsman gives us a dash as he cuts a dash:
Cézanne,
the Zulu of the Brush,
Daumier,
the anatomist of the lawyer's mouth,
Hogarth,
the engraver of harlots for cash.

O Ushas,
I could unweave
a Gobelin arras of irony on graybeard artists
disoriented like Degas when forced to leave
the rue Victor Masse—to make again
a new place for new things and new men.

Black Boy,
White Boy,
out of chaos the dread hand designed
the oval lilac shape
of the rich sweet Tokay;
contrived the helmet-like head of the Cape
buffalo with its diablerie
curved outward, downward, and backward—
then, forward, upward, and inward:
neither man nor beast may hope to escape
when the alarm of the buffalo bird
sets the vicious circle of horns surrealistically flying.

The ape of God
(mind instinct with design)
pricks in the skin of the seafarer's arm
the painted Tyrean form
of the huzzy thrown from a window to the dogs;
blazons the red pallets on the gold
of Aragon's shield;
contrives the triple-rhyming oblong leaf
of the metaphor-maker of Naishapur;
fashions the undulant mold
of the *cyma reversa;*
patterns the mosaics in the baptistries
of San Vitale at Ravenna;
traces the multiple complexities
of shafting in black Purbeckian marble;
fabricates the mordant trill of the grand
pianoforte's warble.

White Boy,
Black Boy,
freedom is the oxygen
of the studio and gallery.
What if a *chef-d'oeuvre* is esoteric?
The cavernous By Room, with its unassignable variety
of ego-dwarfing
stalactites and stalagmites,
makes my veins and arteries vibrate faster
as I study its magnificence and intricacy.
Is it amiss or odd
if the apes of God
take a cue from their Master?

Do not scholars tear their beards—vex
their disciples over the Palestinian and Byzantine
punctuation of the Masoretic texts?

As for the critic,
he is the fid
that bolsters the topmost mast
of Art—an argosy of plunder
from the kingdoms of race and class and caste.
Now and then a State,
when iron fists and hobnails
explode alarms at the citadel's gate,
dons the ill-fitting robes of the Medici
and initiates Project CX,
to propagandize a rubber-stamped pyramid of Art
and to glorify the Cheops at the apex.

Black Boy,
White Boy,
Doctor Nkomo used to dream:
"God's ape
from Giverney gives us new roads
out of the Jardin d'Eau and across the anthroposcape.
If I had the alchemy
of the camel's hair, I'd do, with nuance-by-nuance variety,
as regards
site and trait and light,
a series in a character-history,
like *Cliffs of Etzetat, Coins of Rivière*.
O fruits of the first Harlem harvest,
let the beholder who is neither kith nor kin
recompose the unexpected tones in a dusky Everyman
the painter's brush has disassociated against the milieu—
then boned and fleshed and veined again."

I confess without regret
in this omega of my education:
I no longer have the force of a gilbert,
nor have I ever had the levitation
to sustain a work of art.
I have only pilgrimed
to the cross street
(a godsend in God's acre)
where
curator and creator
meet—
friend yoked to friend at the candle end.

White Boy,
Black Boy,
like the flatted third and seventh notes
in a 12-bar blues,
the identity of the Negro is groovy
in all-God's-children-got shoes.
The moving finger in the Harlem Gallery
paints dramatis personae in the dusk of dawn,
between America's epigraph and epitaph;
yet,
only half an eye has the other half
of the Great White World,
where,
at the crack of doom,
potbellies bellylaugh.

Sometimes the Harlem Gallery
is a harvesting machine without binding
twine; again, a clock that stops
for want of winding:
it is then that the millstones of the Regents
exhaust summer and winter
in grinding
the spirit of The Curator.
But
I envision the Harlem Gallery of my people,
and
(in spite of sounding brass)
I hear the words of Archbishop Trench:
"The present is only intelligible in the light of the past."

Black Boy,
White Boy,
no Haroun-al-Rashid greets the Harlem avant-garde;
in the travailing
dusk of dawn,
a flailing
gibberish may turn one ill-smelling and pale
as characin,
may leave one quailing,
until one discovers it is a
lonely, flailing 666—only
a monkey with a lion's tail.
No Lenox Avenue bar
a-moaning the blues,
no hetaera star
aglitter in the Harlem Opera House,
the day's travel unended and with the night's blended—
I do not expect to hear a Selika's invisible choir
anthem the felicities
of the Beyond's equalizing bar
with its whiffletrees.

Since men of good will are depressed like the rostrum
of the deep-sea Harriotta, since the world's grief
goes unexplained like the why
of the *kind gallows* at Crieff—
send francs (bucks), not *Illuminations*,
to the Afroamerican Djami,
the Harlem Gallery's
faithful Harrari.

White Boy,
Black Boy,
what if this Harlem Exhibition becomes
a *cause célèbre?* The Deluge! I
have no Noah's ark,
no peak of Ararat, to defy
the dusky Regents who,
tasteless as oxygen,
as colorless, too,
can knot the golden purse strings,
while closeted in the Great Amen,
and mix the ingredients of Syncorax' brew!

In the black ghetto
the white heather
and the white almond grow,
but the hyacinth
and asphodel blow
in the white metropolis!
O Cleobulus,
O Thales, Solon, Periander, Bias, Chilo,
O Pittacus,
unriddle the phoenix riddle of this?

Our public may possess in Art
a Mantegna figure's arctic rigidity;
yet—I hazard—yet,
this allegro of the Harlem Gallery
is not a chippy fire,
for here, in focus, are paintings that chronicle
a people's New World odyssey
from chattel to Esquire!